LUKE–ACTS

Donald Juel

SCM PRESS LTD

Copyright © John Knox Press 1983

All rights reserved. No part of this publication may be
reproduced, stored in a retrieval system, or transmitted,
in any form or by any means, electronic, mechanical,
photocopying, recording or otherwise, without the prior
permission of the publisher, SCM Press Ltd.

*Unless otherwise indicated scripture quotations are from
the Revised Standard Version of the Bible, copyright
1946, 1952 and © 1971, 1973 by the Division of Christian
Education, National Council of the Churches of Christ in
America, and used by permission.*

334 00941 3

First British edition published 1984
by SCM Press Ltd
26–30 Tottenham Road, London N1 4BZ

Typeset in the United States of America
and printed in Great Britain by
Richard Clay (The Chaucer Press) Ltd
Bungay, Suffolk

To My Wife

CONTENTS

INTRODUCTION

The two volumes entitled The Gospel According to St. Luke and The Acts of the Apostles dominate the landscape of the New Testament. They comprise almost one-fourth its total verses. Together they represent the most ambitious literary undertaking within the fledgling Christian movement of the first century. Not surprisingly, the two books have left their mark on the life of the church. Jesus' birth in an animal stall, the song of the angels, and the visit of shepherds are features of our Christmas story that Luke alone provides. Mary's *Magnificat,* Zechariah's *Benedictus,* and Simeon's *Nunc Dimittis* are among Luke's contributions to the church's liturgical heritage. The festivals of Pentecost and Ascension owe their place on the ecclesiastical calendar to Acts. Most of our knowledge about the life of the earliest church stems from the tales about Peter and Stephen and Paul. Though we possess several letters written by Paul, it would be fair to say that the image of the great apostle familiar to most people emerges not from his letters but from the colorful stories in Acts.

The Gospel and Acts, both of which bear titles that were not original to the works,[1] were conceived as a unified literary enterprise by their author. Both were dedicated to someone known as Theophilus. From an early date, however, the two books were read as separate volumes. Luke's Gospel was included among the other Gospels. Acts was included in the canon, but as an exceptional work; it was neither a Gospel nor an Epistle, categories by which the church sought to arrange the New Testament writings. The existence of a "wild" textual tradition among certain Greek

1

manuscripts of Acts, in which numerous changes were made with little respect for original wording, may indicate that Acts was not viewed as "scriptural" until some time later than other New Testament writings.[2]

It is not difficult to understand why the Gospel and Acts have been read independently through the history of the church. In efforts to justify the precise selection of works included in the canon, categories like "Gospel" and "Epistle" were helpful. Further, holistic interpretation of biblical narratives has never characterized the tradition. Even today few people read Gospels or letters as units. Moreover, there are striking differences between the Gospel and Acts. The style varies considerably: in the Gospel, Jesus speaks in parables or in aphoristic pronouncements; in Acts, major characters deliver lengthy, complex speeches. The sources are different for each volume. For his Gospel, Luke had literary precedent; for Acts, he apparently had none. Finally, general commentary format and the sheer bulk of material in the Lukan corpus have impeded unified interpretation even when scholars have recognized its appropriateness.

Henry Cadbury was a grand exception in the history of Lukan scholarship. Cadbury, a distinguished professor of New Testament at Harvard, insisted that the two volumes be interpreted as part of a common endeavor. His *The Making of Luke-Acts* is a classic, required reading for any serious student of the New Testament.[3] Following his lead, recent Lukan scholarship has broken with centuries of tradition by reading the Gospel and Acts together. Cadbury's hyphenated "Luke-Acts" is employed as an indication that the two volumes must be read as an entity.

This little volume is an introduction to Luke-Acts. With so vast a body of material, I do not feel constrained to say something about everything. The study concentrates on interpretive matters appropriate to Luke-Acts as a whole: why did the author of the Gospel, unlike other evangelists, choose to create a larger framework within which to interpret Jesus' ministry? what difference does it make to our interpretation of the Gospel and Acts that one follows the other? what themes distinguish and/or unite parts one and two of Luke's history? is the unified work of a different genre than either taken individually? It is with such questions that we will be occupied in the course of our study.

Before turning to an analysis of Luke-Acts, there are a few introductory matters that warrant brief consideration. The first has to do with the sources of Luke's writings.

Traditions in Luke-Acts

Scholars who study Luke and Acts acknowledge that the two works are very different even if written by the same author. Luke was far more limited in his composition of the Gospel than of Acts. He had precedent for his story of Jesus (Luke 1:1); however, no one had written an account of the apostles' mission. Here the author was moving through uncharted waters, and although he may have had sources at his disposal, it is far more difficult to isolate them. Methods of interpretation that depend upon identification of sources as a means of assessing the author's intention have been relatively unsuccessful. Luke may have had sources for Acts, but they are difficult to detect.[4]

Sources of the Gospel are more easily identifiable. Luke is characterized as one of the "Synoptic Gospels." For more than a century, scholars have studied Matthew, Mark, and Luke together, using a synopsis in which the three are arranged in parallel columns. Even without a synopsis readers can appreciate the great similarities among the works; the story line is the same, with the exception of the beginnings and endings. Jesus' ministry divides neatly into a Galilean and a Jerusalem phase. In the three Gospels, Jesus is portrayed as an exorcist with extraordinary power, a religious maverick who confounds his pious countrymen by associating with sinners, as a popular teacher at home in the idiom of the common people. The use of a synopsis reveals even more striking agreements, however. Not only are stories similar, but words, sentences, sometimes whole passages, are identical.

Virtually everyone who has studied the "synoptic problem," the relationship among Matthew, Mark, and Luke, has agreed that some literary relationship among the three is the only satisfactory explanation for the patterns of agreement and disagreement. Either one or more of the evangelists used one or more of the others as a source, or all employed a common source (or sources), now lost.

The problem is complex, which is perhaps the reason there is at the moment no scholarly consensus about the synoptic problem. A majority of scholars still defends the notion of Markan priority, i.e., the thesis that Mark's Gospel was the first and that it was used as a source by both Matthew and Luke. Markan priority would account for some of the material Matthew and Luke have in common while also explaining individual agreements between Matthew and Mark and Luke and Mark when corresponding material is lacking in the third Gospel. Those who defend Markan priority must also postulate a second source comprised of sayings of Jesus, used independently by Matthew and Luke, since the two Gospels share extensive teaching material not found in Mark. The hypothetical sayings source is known as "Q" (for the German "Quelle," which means simply "source"). According to this theory, Matthew and Luke each had access to special material as well as to Mark and "Q." The relationship is diagrammed in the following way:

SPECIAL M ⟶ MATTHEW ⟵ MARK ⟶ LUKE ⟵ SPECIAL L
     Q

The theory has never lacked critics, and new studies appear regularly advocating the priority of Matthew, exposing flaws in previous theories. Those interested in the problem can find ample discussion in introductions and in monographs.[5] I will assume Markan priority in this volume.

Luke's Gospel is derivative in an important sense. He depended not only on "eyewitnesses and ministers of the word" but on written sources. His history is revisionist, an attempt to improve what had preceded (though the sense in which he intended to improve on his predecessors is yet to be determined). One method of study, widely practiced among biblical critics, is to examine carefully how Luke made use of his sources. If he employed Mark's Gospel and a collection of Jesus' sayings as his primary sources, we can observe in detail how he worked: how did he modify wording? where did he make additions? in what places did he rearrange scenes or supply new punch lines? Such an approach is possible only if there is agreement about Luke's sources, of course, but even without such agreement we can appreciate the subtle differences between Luke and his co-evangelists.

Reconstruction of sources is only one approach, however, and it promises more success to the student of Luke's Gospel than to the student of Acts. An exclusive focus on sources, moreover, may detract from the finished product, obscuring the continuity between parts one and two of Luke's history. It may account for differences between the two volumes, but it cannot pass for a sufficient explanation or for adequate interpretation.

Author, Date, and Setting

In one respect this is not the place to discuss who wrote Luke-Acts at what time and in what setting, since the only real evidence we possess for making such determinations lies within the works themselves. Because assumptions about author, date, and setting influence interpretation, however, a few preliminary comments are necessary.

The persistence of the traditional ascription of the two volumes to "Luke the beloved physician" is balanced by the almost total lack of supporting evidence. The name "Luke" occurs in neither volume. The title "The Gospel According to St. Luke" was certainly not part of the original manuscript,[6] which makes it virtually useless as evidence.

If the name "Luke" came to be associated with the volumes, identification of the author as one of Paul's coworkers and as a physician would have been natural in light of references in Paul's letters:

> Epaphras, my fellow prisoner in Christ Jesus, sends greetings to you, and so do Mark, Aristarchus, Demas, and Luke, my fellow workers. (Philemon 23–24)

> Luke the beloved physician and Demas greet you. (Col. 4:14)

> Do your best to come to me soon. For Demas, in love with this present world, has deserted me and gone to Thessalonica; Crescens has gone to Galatia, Titus to Dalmatia. Luke alone is with me. (2 Tim. 4:9–11)

There is some evidence that the author of Acts traveled with Paul. In Acts 16, the narrator suddenly shifts from third person to first person:

> And they went through the region of Phrygia and Galatia, having been forbidden by the Holy Spirit to speak the word in Asia. And when they had come opposite Mysia. . . . And a vision appeared to Paul in the night. . . . And when he had seen the vision, immediately we sought to go on into Macedonia, concluding that God had called us to preach the gospel to them. (Acts 16:6–10)

From this point on, "we" moves in and out of the story, often without notice and always without explanation. The natural inference is that the narrator traveled with Paul during some of his voyages. That inference gives rise to new problems, however. There are frequent tensions between material in Acts about Paul and parallel material in Paul's letters; sometimes there are genuine contradictions.[7] It is difficult to account for some of the discrepancies in the theory that Acts was written by an intimate of Paul. Some have theorized that the "we-passages" derive from a diary kept by a companion of Paul to which the author of Acts had access. The inability of scholars to distinguish stylistically between the so-called travel narrative and other portions of Acts may indicate that the author worked over his source. It may also indicate that the author and the keeper of the diary were the same person. The evidence is inconclusive, which is why so many diverse interpretations have been offered.

Even if Acts was written by someone who traveled with Paul, he is nowhere identified as "Luke." If there is little evidence that someone named Luke wrote the two volumes, there is less reason to regard the author as a physician. As Henry Cadbury demonstrated in his doctoral dissertation decades ago, Luke's use of medical terminology is paralleled in the writings of other authors and historians. The technical vocabulary tells us more about the care and sophistication of the writer than it does about his occupation.[8]

Who wrote the volumes we know as Luke-Acts? In my judgment the question cannot be answered with a name. I will refer to the author as Luke for convenience, but I consider it unlikely that our

"Luke" was a physician who traveled with Paul. We will have opportunity to consider the matter more fully later.

If we do not know the author's name, we know something about him. He displays the greatest literary skill of any of the evangelists and is probably the only one with any literary pretensions. It is conceivable that he intended his works to be published. The author is a third-generation believer, familiar not only with traditions from "eye-witnesses and ministers of the word" but also with written stories about Jesus (Luke 1:1–4). The narratives may also provide surprises. Tradition pictures Luke as a Gentile. I am presently inclined to view him as a Jew, or at least as a proselyte to Judaism. Since evidence for such views depends upon interpretation of the narratives, this question too can be deferred.

The dating of Luke-Acts is less problematic. Luke's Gospel was written after Mark's. Acts was written after the Gospel. If Mark's Gospel was written shortly after 70 C.E., as recent studies suggest,[9] Luke-Acts could not have been written earlier. Conclusive evidence for dating, if such exists, relates to events surrounding the destruction of the temple in 70 C.E. and to subsequent developments within the Jewish community. The two volumes together and Acts in particular seem to mirror events between 80–95 C.E. as they are presently understood by historians. Arguments must await interpretation of the relevant passages. To anticipate, it seems likely that Luke and Acts were written between 80–90 C.E.

One complication has a bearing on dating the two volumes. It is not certain that the Gospel and Acts were written in close succession. Though Jesus' last words in Luke 24 anticipate Acts and the opening verses in Acts refer to the Gospel, there are differences. In the Gospel, Jesus' ascent to heaven occurs on Easter Sunday (Luke 24:51). In Acts, Jesus spends forty days with his followers prior to his ascension (Acts 1:3). One possible explanation is that Luke wrote Acts several years after writing the Gospel. Forgetfulness seems an unlikely explanation for the discrepancies, however. Other explanations are equally, if not more, plausible.[10] There may even be grounds to suspect that someone tampered with the ending of the Gospel to make it more suitable as an independent volume. Though the problems cannot be ignored, they cannot obscure the essential unity of Luke and Acts.

Where were the two volumes composed? Again, there is little hard evidence for a decision. If the books were written by Paul's companion, Rome may seem a likely setting for their composition, since "we" occurs in the concluding chapter in Acts that tells of Paul's arrival in the imperial capital. Others have suggested Ephesus or Antioch; still others advocate a city in Macedonia or Achaia.[11] There is no scholarly consensus, and without further data there probably never will be. We may agree on a profile of the community for which Luke wrote, but probably not on its location.

Virtually none of the important questions we might ask of Luke-Acts can be answered in advance. Tradition offers answers, but they are no less dependent upon inference and conjecture than our own. We are left with Luke's writings. What we learn we will learn largely from our engagement with the narratives. It is to that task that we now turn.

CHAPTER I

Beginnings

The first two chapters in Luke's Gospel are remarkable in many respects. First, Luke is the only one of the evangelists to tell his audience anything in advance about the story he is about to recount. The narrative is prefaced with a four-verse introduction or proem, and this has considerable bearing on our interpretation of Luke-Acts. These chapters also contain material which is unique to Luke. With the exception of Mary and Joseph, none of the characters appears in other Gospels, and most—Zechariah, Elizabeth, the shepherds, Simeon, and Anna—play no further role in the story; in fact, they are never mentioned again. Hymnic outbursts by Mary, Zechariah, and Simeon are confined to these chapters; the style and even the vocabulary of these hymns are distinctive.

These chapters have been the subject of considerable debate. In the recent past, prominent students of Luke-Acts argued that the chapters did not really belong with the rest of the Gospel or Acts.[1] Some interpretations of Luke's Gospel completely ignored the birth narratives, Mary's *Magnificat,* and Zechariah's *Benedictus.* Few scholars today, however, are persuaded by these arguments. Most consider the first two chapters an integral part of the Gospel, though no particular interpretation holds sway.[2]

We will begin our study of Luke-Acts by examining the first two chapters of the Gospel. Particularly because the material is unique to Luke, analysis of these chapters should provide a good introduction to Luke's version of Jesus' story, perhaps even to his history of the early church. Themes identified in these chapters and questions that emerge from our study of them will provide a structure for the rest of this volume.

Prefaces

Prefaces to literary works were common for certain types of writing. Comparison of Luke's prefaces (or proems) to the Gospel and Acts with prefaces to works written by his contemporaries can be instructive. The following are prefaces to two volumes written by the Jewish historian, Josephus, a contemporary of Luke.[3] I have included the appropriate verses from Luke's Gospel and Acts in parallel columns for convenience.

"Against Apion" (Josephus)

In my history of Antiquities most excellent Epaphroditus, I have, I think, made sufficiently clear to any who may peruse that work the extreme antiquity of our Jewish race. ... Since, however, I observe that a considerable number of persons, influenced by the malicious calumnies of certain individuals, discredit the statements in my history concerning our antiquity. ... I consider it my duty to devote a brief treatise to all these points; in order at once to convict our detractors of malignity and deliberate falsehood, to correct the ignorance of others, and to instruct all who desire to know the truth concerning the antiquity of our race.

In the first volume of this work, my most esteemed Epaphroditus, I demonstrated the antiquity of our race. ... I shall now proceed to refute the rest of the authors who have attacked us.

Luke 1:1–4

Inasmuch as many have undertaken to compile a narrative of the things which have been accomplished among us, just as they were delivered to us by those who from the beginning were eyewitnesses and ministers of the word, it seemed good to me also, having followed all things closely for some time past, to write an orderly account for you, most excellent Theophilus, that you may know the truth concerning the things of which you have been informed.

Acts 1:1–2

In the first book, O Theophilus, I have dealt with all that Jesus began to do and teach, until the day when he was taken up, after he had given commandment through the Holy Spirit to the apostles whom he had chosen.

Thus Josephus and Luke introduce their respective works. Such prefaces, or proems, provide the reader important clues about the nature of the writing. For the first-century reader such clues were perhaps more important than for us. Today an author communicates literary intent in many ways. The arrangement of a poem on the printed page tells us to expect imaginative writing rather than journalism. The texture of newsprint, the arrangement of articles in columns, and the use of different-sized type mean we are to expect news reporting—a genre distinct from "editorials," which we hope to find clearly marked. Each type of writing demands a different set of expectations from readers. Authors and readers operate within a world of convention in which whole sets of interpretive rubrics can be assumed.

Ancient writers were no less conventional than contemporary writers, but they were more limited in their means of communication. Their writing material was usually papyrus or animal skins; they printed their text in capital letters, in columns, and without punctuation. Works sometimes appeared without titles, often lacking also the name of the author. The titles "Gospel According to Luke" and "Acts of the Apostles" were certainly not original; "gospel" was not even a category of literature in antiquity. The proems to the Gospel of Luke and the Acts of the Apostles may thus represent more significant clues to the rubrics appropriate to the literature than the present titles.

Luke's proem suggests that the author has literary pretensions. Though scholars disagree to some extent, it seems that the dedication of the work to Theophilus, like Josephus' dedication of his work to Epaphroditus, intends to insure publication of the material. Epaphroditus, Josephus' patron, was apparently a teacher of note, owner of a considerable library, and above all, wealthy enough to underwrite copying and distribution of "Against Apion." Dedication to an individual may well imply a desire to make public the writing. If so, the author of the two volumes dedicated to Theophilus would be the only New Testament author to state his intention to enter the world of letters. The elegant Greek and the carefully balanced structure of the proem to Luke's Gospel support such a conjecture.

Another observation is that in Luke and Acts, as in "Against Apion," one literary whole is divided into two parts, with volume two prefaced by a secondary introduction. Since writing in the first century was done on scrolls, and since a limit was imposed on the length of a scroll, longer works required division into discrete "volumes." Scholars have determined that the Gospel of Luke and the Acts would each fill a normal scroll. Though there is some disagreement, the simplest explanation for the separation of the two volumes is size. The short rededication to Theophilus and introduction to Acts, with some brief reference to the preceding volume, would have been required at the beginning of a new and separate scroll. The practice seems conventional. That means, however, that the two books should be viewed as two parts of one literary unit, despite their separation in the present canon of the New Testament. This also places the writings in a special class. Luke is the only known Christian in the first or second century to combine the story of Jesus with the story of the early church.

Finally, the proem tells us something about the nature of the composition: it falls within the category of history-writing. By referring to "narratives" and "orderly accounts," and by making statements about predecessors and sources, Luke tells us something about his writings that other evangelists do not about theirs. He informs the reader that what follows is not a poem, not a philosophical treatise, not a series of essays on the moral life, not a collection of letters, not a commentary on the Bible—all of which were options for Luke. Examples of such types of literature are found in Jewish and Christian writings contemporary with Luke-Acts. The author, however, regards himself as a historian; his narrative will recount events in a sequence, events which have significance and which cohere in some recognizable way.

Luke was not the only ancient to see connections among human events and to attempt a history. Historiography was widely practiced among his contemporaries, widely discussed by historians, and even taught in schools. Discussion of the use of speeches in histories by the historians Polybius and Thucydides, Lucian's essay, "How to Write History," and the wide range of ancient histories can provide information about shared expectations of author and audience in antiquity. Study of Luke's contemporaries may shed light on the structure of his work or on aspects of his style. Knowing the extraordinary effort devoted to the composition of speeches by historiographers and the functions of the speeches in their histories, we can understand why all the major characters in Acts deliver speeches at crucial junctures in the story, speeches that bear the earmarks of careful composition.[4] If Luke does set out to write history, there is much we can learn from his contemporaries about what "history" and history-writing meant to people living in the Graeco-Roman world in the first century.

Luke-Acts must be studied in its setting in the Graeco-Roman world. The author writes not about the history of the Empire, however, but about a particular series of events that involve principally Jews, especially Jews who have come into contact with Jesus of Nazareth. Luke places his literary effort in a framework provided by "eyewitnesses and ministers of the word." Luke is, if we may use the term, the first Christian historian. Such an assertion prompts questions: what led this author to tie together the stories of Jesus and stories of his followers after his ascension, particularly when others like Matthew, Mark, and John did not? why this precise selection of events? what threads tie together the parents of John the Baptist and tales of Paul's voyages around the Mediterranean? Diodorus Siculus set out to chronicle the history of Rome; Josephus wrote several volumes recounting events that led to the disastrous war against Rome in A.D. 66–73; centuries later, Eusebius wrote a history of the church explaining its inexorable progress toward imperial recognition under Constantine. What story does Luke set out to tell? Where does it begin and where does it end? Josephus writes, he tells us, to combat errors and to defend himself and his people against slanders. What motivates the author of Luke-Acts to produce two volumes for Theophilus? It is possible that the proem will help answer such questions.

The major introduction to Luke-Acts occurs in Luke 1:1–4. Although the preface introduces the Gospel, we will not be far wrong in reading it as a statement about the two-volume work as a whole.[5] These four verses are among the most carefully crafted in the New Testament. The Greek is elegant and quite distinct from the prose that follows. The verses comprise a carefully balanced statement. In view of the author's careful formulation and the importance of wording, four English versions of the proem are included, since, as we shall see, translators differ considerably about what the verses say.

> Inasmuch as many have undertaken to compile a narrative of the things which have been accomplished among us, just as they were delivered to us by those who from the beginning were eyewitnesses and ministers of the word, it seemed good to me also, having followed all things closely for some time past, to write an orderly account for you, most excellent Theophilus, that you may know the truth concerning the things of which you have been informed. (RSV)

> Many writers have undertaken to draw up an account of the events that have happened among us, following the traditions handed down to us by the original eyewitnesses and servants of the Gospel. And so I in my turn, your Excellency, as one who has gone over the whole course of these events in detail, have decided to write a connected narrative for you so as to give you authentic knowledge about the matters of which you have been informed. (NEB)

> Many have undertaken to draw up an account of the things that have been fulfilled among us, just as they were handed down to us by those who from the first were eyewitnesses and servants of the word. Therefore, since I myself have carefully investigated everything from the beginning, it seems good also to me to write an orderly account for you, most excellent Theophilus, so that you may know the certainty of the things you have been taught. (NIV)

> Seeing that many others have undertaken to draw up accounts of the events that have taken place among us, exactly as they were handed down to us by those who from the outset were eyewitnesses and ministers of the word, I in my turn, after carefully going over the whole story from the beginning, have decided to write an ordered account for you, Theophilus, so that your Excellency may learn how well founded the teaching is that you have received. (JB)

About the author there is no disagreement among the translations. Though he does not give his name, he does inform his readers that he is not a first-generation Christian. What he writes has been handed down by "eyewitnesses and ministers of the

word." He gives no names. Furthermore, the author is not the first
to write about Jesus. "Many," he tells us, have written about the
events he will recount. We know of two such writers: the author of
The Gospel According to Mark, and the author (or authors) of a
collection of Jesus' sayings, known as "Q."[6] Luke's reference to
"many" may be conventional.

The translations also agree about the designated recipient: he is
called Theophilus, a name meaning "friend of God," not
uncommon in Jewish or Graeco-Roman society. We do not know
Theophilus. Some believe he was an official, in which case the
Greek word *kratistos* could be translated "your excellency." Others
disagree, pointing out that the Greek term may simply be used in
polite address (Josephus refers to Epaphroditus as "most
excellent"). More important is what we learn of Theophilus in the
last verse: he has "been informed." Again, options are available to
translators. The term may mean simply "informed"; it may also be
translated "taught" or "instructed." The term is used in Acts 18:25
to refer to Christian instruction. Later the word becomes a technical
term for religious instruction (our English words "to catechize" and
"catechism" come from the Greek term). Is Theophilus an official
who has heard about Jesus and his followers, or is he a believer who
has "been instructed" in the faith? Both interpretations are
possible. One reading might suggest that Luke-Acts is intended as
political apologetic or perhaps as missionary literature; another
might suggest it was written primarily for believers.

The crucial phrase for understanding Luke's intent is in verse 4.
Once again translations differ. Does Luke write so that his readers
will know "the truth" (RSV), implying that they do not possess the
truth? The NEB appears to follow this line even more consistently:
Luke seeks to provide "authentic knowledge." Josephus' comments about his work suggest such an interpretation: he writes to set
the record straight, to correct misinformation and to combat
outright lies. According to the JB and NIV, however, Luke writes to
instill confidence and security: "so that you may hear how well
founded the teaching is" (JB) or "so that you may know the
certainty" (NIV). According to this view, Luke seeks to persuade,
not necessarily to correct. If this rendering of the Greek is more

appropriate, as I would argue, and if the projected reader has "been instructed" as a Christian, as I shall argue below, several questions arise. What kinds of doubts might believers have about the story of Jesus or about the history of his followers? Why tell the story again for people who have heard "many" other versions? Without assuming that early Christians were preoccupied with "heretics," as were later church leaders, is there evidence that Luke wrote against certain views or with particular problems in mind? Such questions will occupy us throughout this volume.

One additional comment. The same Greek work in verse 1 is variously translated "accomplished," "happened," "taken place," or "fulfilled." The word is not the ordinary term for "happen" or "occur." The RSV and the NIV aptly note the presence of the root "to fulfill." The word "fulfill" suggests that the events which have transpired are not mere occurrences: rather, they fill up or fill out something; they reach toward some goal, which would suggest this story cannot be read by itself. The events belong in some larger context; they are perhaps part of a plan. The Greek word, so read, is an appropriate introduction to Luke's history.

Great Expectations: Luke 1—2

Each Gospel writer begins the story of Jesus in the writer's own way. Mark begins in the middle of things, with John the Baptist's career in full swing and Jesus already an adult. Matthew opens with a genealogy and stories about Jesus' birth. The fourth Gospel traces the story back to the dawn of creation: "In the beginning." In Luke, however, the story opens in Jerusalem with a country priest and his wife. Details are sparse: we learn only that Zechariah and Elizabeth are exemplary Jews and that they are in the holy city because Zechariah's division of the priesthood is on duty at the temple. (When not on duty in the temple, most priests lived outside the city.) In other respects there is nothing extraordinary about the two characters or their lives.

The action begins in the temple, where Zechariah is about to officiate at the burning of incense, a privilege accorded priests only once in their lives. The choice of this priest "by lot" is no coincidence, we learn. This most holy place is the proper setting for a visit from an angel which has been planned. A heavenly messenger announces that Zechariah and Elizabeth, though beyond the age of conceiving and bearing children, will have a son. Gabriel's solemn canticle anticipates the decisive role the child will play in God's plan of salvation: he will make ready for the Lord "a people prepared," fulfilling the tasks assigned Elijah the prophet, whose return had long been awaited by faithful Jews (Malachi 4:5–6). Zechariah and his contemporaries stand on the threshold of a new day; the aging couple have an important role to play in the momentous events to come.

The heavenly visit, we learn, was no illusion. The incredulous Zechariah is struck dumb for his lack of faith, which leads worshipers to believe that he has seen a vision. In fulfillment of the angel's promise, Elizabeth conceives a child. Meanwhile, further interventions occur, more remarkable than the first. Gabriel appears again, this time to a young girl with no apparent pedigree or status. He announces that she has been selected by God to bear a son who will inherit the throne of David and who will reign over Israel forever. The child, she is told, will be born without a human father. The Most High himself will see to the conception, so that the child will aptly be called "the Son of God." God has begun to fulfill ancient promises; Zechariah, Elizabeth, and Mary are agents of changes that will alter the course of history.

In many respects, the story of Jesus the Christ and Son of God opens as readers in the Graeco-Roman world would have expected. Stories about the marvelous births of heroes and kings and even philosophers abounded. Whether recounting the miraculous nature of conception (Plato, Alexander the Great, and Augustus were among the many alleged to have been born of a union of a god and a mortal woman) or the auspicious signs accompanying the birth of the savior-to-be, infancy stories testified to the extraordinary nature of the child. Here are a few stories culled from legends about two famous "saviors" from antiquity, Alexander and Augustus:

> Alexander was a descendent of Herakles, on his father's side, through Karanos; on his mother's side he was descended from Aikos through Neoptolemos. . . .

The bride [Alexander's mother], before the night in which they were to join in the bridechamber, had a vision. There was a peal of thunder, and a lightning bolt fell upon her womb. A great fire was kindled from the strike, then it broke into flames which flashed everywhere, then they extinguished. At a later time, after the marriage, Philip [Alexander's father] saw a vision: he was placing a seal on his wife's womb; the engraving on the seal was, as he thought, in the image of a lion. . . .

In the book, *Theologumenon* by Asclepias of Mendes, I read that when Atia [Augustus' mother] had come in the middle of the night to the solemn rite of Apollo, when her litter had been set in the temple, and while the other women slept, . . . she slept. A snake slipped up to her and, after a little while, went out. When she awoke, she purified herself as if coming from her husband's bed. And immediately on her body there appeared a mark colored like a snake, and she could never get rid of it. . . . Augustus was born in the tenth month after this and because of this was considered the son of Apollo.

Atia herself, before she gave birth to him, dreamed that her womb was carried up to the stars and spread out all over the earth and sky. Octavius, the father, dreamed that the radiance of the sun rose from Atia's womb.

When Octavius led an army through the remote regions of Thrace, he consulted about his son with barbarian rites in the grove of Father Liber. [Augustus' future reign] was confirmed by the priests, because when the wine was poured on the altar such a great flame shot up that it went beyond the roof of the temple to the sky. Only in the case of Alexander the Great, when he offered a sacrifice on the same altar, did a like portent occur.

Similarities in Luke extend even to terminology. Jesus, like Alexander, Augustus, and other Caesars, is called "savior," as well as Son of God. The opening chapters in the Gospel are filled with wondrous appearances and startling messages from heavenly beings. Old people conceive a child; a virgin bears a son; shepherds are entertained by the host of heaven; simple people—Zechariah, Elizabeth, Mary, and Simeon—are inspired by the Holy Spirit and utter prophecies. The two babes, John and Jesus, born because of heaven's intervention, are no ordinary mortals. The world will be different because of their births.

It is all the more remarkable, therefore, what small roles major political and religious figures play in these events. The author is not unaware of their presence: Herod is king of Judea, Quirinius is governor of Syria, Augustus is in power in Rome. The story is not about them, however—at least, not yet. The actors are simple folk: an ordinary priest and his aging wife; a young peasant woman; a Jew named Joseph who, like other descendants of the great King David, must now bend to the will of Caesar and pay taxes; shepherds, a despised class in Jewish society; an old man (Simeon); and an aged widow (Anna). Kings and chief priests play no role at all. Jesus' birth is ignored by a world busy with its own affairs; the actual event occurs in an animal stall because there is no room elsewhere. The career of the young king will eventually intersect with those of governors and religious officials, but for now he belongs with the simple and the poor.

Stories about marvelous births were common to Jewish as well as to Graeco-Roman tradition. Jews never spoke of sexual unions between their God and mortal women, but they readily spoke of God's involvement in the conception of children. Genesis tells how God fulfilled the promise of a son to Abraham and Sarah. Isaac was conceived long after the couple could expect children. His birth was seen as a gift from God. In a story with numerous parallels to that of John's and Jesus' births, the narrator of 1 Samuel recounts the remarkable birth of a son to Hannah, who, upon bearing a child in answer to her prayers, sings a song of praise to God highly reminiscent of Mary's song (1 Sam. 2:1–10 and Luke 1:46–55):

> Hannah also prayed and said,
>   "My heart exults in the LORD;
>   my strength is exalted in the LORD.
> My mouth derides my enemies,
>   because I rejoice in thy salvation.
>
> "There is none holy like the LORD,
>   there is none besides thee;
>   there is no rock like our God.

Talk no more so very proudly,
  let not arrogance come from your mouth;
for the LORD is a God of knowledge,
  and by him actions are weighed.
The bows of the mighty are broken,
  but the feeble gird on strength.
Those who were full have hired themselves out for bread,
  but those who were hungry have ceased to hunger.
The barren has borne seven,
  but she who has many children is forlorn.
The LORD kills and brings to life;
  he brings down to Sheol and raises up.
The LORD makes poor and makes rich;
  he brings low, he also exalts.
He raises up the poor from the dust;
  he lifts the needy from the ash heap,
to make them sit with princes
  and inherit a seat of honor.
For the pillars of the earth are the LORD's,
  and on them he has set the world.

"He will guard the feet of his faithful ones;
  but the wicked shall be cut off in darkness;
  for not by might shall a man prevail.
The adversaries of the LORD shall be broken to pieces;
  against them he will thunder in heaven.
The LORD will judge the ends of the earth;
  he will give strength to his king,
  and exalt the power of his anointed." (1 Sam. 2:1–10)

Most Old Testament scholars believe that the hymn attributed to Hannah originated elsewhere; its placement in the narrative derives from a storyteller who sensed in the experience of this ordinary woman some insight into the working of Israel's God.

The hymns and prophetic outbursts of various characters in Luke's story have the same function. They are appropriate to the situation, yet they offer an interpretation of events that both foreshadows what is to come and relates them to promises and motifs familiar from Israel's past. The hymns provide an interpretive framework within which the entire story can be understood. That they are unique to Luke only makes these songs all the more significant for interpreting his Gospel.

Song of Mary (Luke 1:46–55)

The poem called the *Magnificat* because of the first word of the song in the Latin Bible is reminiscent of Old Testament psalms both in structure and word usage. The parallel with Hannah's song in 1 Samuel is particularly striking. Both songs take God's gift of a son to simple women as a sign of particular concern for the poor and the humble. According to Hannah, God "raises up the poor from the dust"; according to Mary, God "has filled the hungry with good things." "The bows of the mighty are broken," sings Hannah; echoes Mary, God has "put down the mighty from their thrones." The consistent use of the past tense in Mary's hymn perhaps obscures the implication of the Greek: like the prophets of old, Mary can speak of the future that has now begun to unfold with her conception of Jesus as already fulfilled. Her song is not simply a rehearsal of what God has done, but an anticipation of what God will surely do. So certain is Mary, that she can speak of future acts as already accomplished.

The God who chose Mary and Hannah is a God who has consistently been on the side of the lowly and the oppressed. The prophets regularly complained on God's behalf of the poor treatment accorded the fatherless and widows, the poor and the helpless. God does not, however, leave the world to itself. According to the prophets and to Mary, God has "put down the mighty from their thrones and exalted those of low degree"; God has "sent the rich empty away." God subverts established values in the interest of truth and for the sake of the outcast. It is no accident that the cast of characters includes simple people. Their mere presence anticipates important aspects of Jesus' career.

These chapters thus prepare us for Jesus' ministry. His particular concern for outcasts and his conflict with vested interests are consistent with the ways of God as Luke understands them. His parables pronounce judgment on the merciless and greedy and offer hope of reversals in the world to come for their victims. Such themes may cause us to look ahead: how and when will the young king seize power and establish his kingdom? will he discredit governors and priests, and will rulers be torn from their thrones?

One additional feature of Mary's hymn is worthy of note: the anticipated fulfillment of God's promised deliverance is placed squarely within Israel's tradition. The song itself is reminiscent of Old Testament songs; the language is "biblical." Furthermore, Mary sings that God has "helped his servant Israel, in remembrance of his mercy, as he spoke to our fathers, to Abraham and to his posterity for ever." The birth and career of Jesus are neither isolated nor accidental occurrences. They correspond to hopes that are centuries old, to promises made by God to Abraham, the father of the race. Luke's story will be one of continuity as well as surprises, of restoration as well as judgment. Mary's *Magnificat* offers preliminary answers to some of our questions about Luke's history: the story of Jesus and John has a beginning at least, long ago, with promises made by God. The history of Jesus and John is part of the history of God's people Israel.

Song of Zechariah (Luke 1:68–79)

The priest's hymn, uttered under the influence of the Spirit, stresses even more the sense of continuity with the history of God's promise. The hymn itself corresponds to traditional forms of blessing that were part of Israel's worship. God is praised for "raising up a horn of salvation for us in the house of his servant David" (referring to Jesus the Savior). The events in which Zechariah plays a role correspond with what God "spoke by the mouth of his holy prophets from of old"; they were "promised to our fathers." God acts "to remember his holy covenant, the oath which he swore to our father, Abraham." The story will return to this theme again and again. Speeches in Acts will rehearse prophecies and promises God has now fulfilled. Paul's last speech to Jews in Rome will conclude with a quotation from the prophet Isaiah. From beginning to end Luke's history is about God's faithfulness to promises made to the Israelites.

The "salvation" God will accomplish through the savior, Jesus, is not spelled out in detail. It is striking, however, how little is said about certain elements in Israel's dreams of the future. God's promises to Abraham in Genesis, for example, include reference to the land Abraham's heirs will possess as well as to descendants as many as the stars of heaven. During times of bondage many Jews looked forward to the day when that "promised land" would be theirs again. According to Zechariah, the oath God swore to Abraham was more specific:

> to grant us that we, being delivered from the hand of our enemies, might serve him without fear, in holiness and righteousness before him, all the days of our life. (1:74–75)

The word translated "serve" might better be rendered "worship." The oath has a cultic ring, perhaps not surprising coming from a priest. The promise now verging on fulfillment is of unrestricted worship of God. Is there something restricted about worship of God at the moment? The temple, destroyed in 587 B.C., had been rebuilt and later restored by Herod to some of its original splendor. Could one not view its rebuilding, rededication, and refurbishing as the fulfillment of such a promise? Who are "our enemies"? The Romans are the obvious candidates. Yet as the drama unfolds Romans have a small role to play. Jesus, Peter and John, Stephen, and finally Paul will be arrested by temple officials. Chief priests will find the message of Jesus and his emissaries particularly threatening. Are they the enemies?

The story that begins with a vision in the temple will extend to the ends of the earth. The temple and the city of Jerusalem have a central role to play. At this point, however, it is unclear precisely what that role will be. Zechariah's prophecy introduces some question about worship and the temple. It may also serve to redirect expectations. We hear nothing of possessing the land, nothing about the dominion of the king, little to conjure up images of the splendor of King David and Solomon. If there is continuity with the tradition, there are also surprises.

Simeon's Oracle (Luke 2:29–35)

The last of the hymns is sung by Simeon, a holy man "looking for the consolation of Israel," who has been promised he would not die before he had seen the Messiah. Upon seeing the infant Jesus in the temple, Simeon, like Zechariah, blesses God. His testimony is added to that of the heavenly host: Jesus is the promised savior. He adds a new element, however: salvation will be for *all* peoples. Jesus will be a light to Gentiles as well as glory for Israel. In a narrative that has emphasized over and over God's faithfulness to Israel, the inclusion of Gentiles is a genuine addition. It is appropriate, of course, that the phrases in Simeon's outburst derive from Israel's Scriptures (specifically from Isa. 52:10; 42:6; and 49:6). Even salvation for Gentiles belongs within Israel's prophetic heritage. The brief passage anticipates the book of Acts, which will tell how salvation was carried to the ends of the earth.

Simeon introduces another element into the narrative with his brief prophecy to Mary. The coming savior of Israel will not be hailed by everyone; his mission will not be one of unequivocal blessing. He may bring consolation to Israel, but he is "set for the fall" of many in Israel. His advent will precipitate a crisis in which the "thoughts of many hearts will be revealed." The prophecy is interested more in Jesus' impact on insiders than on outsiders. His coming will occasion division within God's own people; Jew will be set against Jew. The reversals God will bring about, heralded by Mary, will occur within the people of God; the "enemies" from whom God will deliver the people may well be enemies within the family. One thing seems clear: the world will not ignore Jesus for long. Conflicts are certain.[8]

The opening chapters provide glimpses of what is to come; they raise many questions as well. In the rest of the volume we will follow up the clues and seek answers to some of the questions.

CHAPTER II

"A Savior Who Is Christ the Lord"

Though Luke and Acts together form a unified literary endeavor, the division between parts one and two is substantial. Part one, the Gospel, tells how the promise of a savior to Israel was fulfilled in the ministry of Jesus. Part two traces the spread of that news to the ends of the earth. It is thus appropriate to examine each part as a unit, while also recognizing their interdependence.

The Anointing

Jesus, the Son of Mary, is introduced as a promising young man. Though most of the world failed to take note of his birth, a few pious souls caught at least a glimpse of what lay ahead. While the narrator does not suggest that Jesus' childhood was unusual, there is at least one premonition of things to come. Like the prophet Samuel, Jesus displayed a sense of vocation beyond his years. Even as a twelve-year-old he understood that the temple was to play a major role in his life. His parents, discovering his absence from the group of townspeople returning from Passover festivities in Jerusalem, retrace their steps only to find their son discussing religious matters with teachers of the law in the temple. "How is it that you sought me?" Jesus asks them. "Did you not know that I must be in my Father's house?" (Luke 2:49).

We learn nothing more about the young man until he has matured, when his reappearance occurs in a surprising manner. The one destined to rule Israel submits to a baptism of repentance for the forgiveness of sins. The story, told with remarkable economy of detail, was problematic for some. Mark's version (1:9–11) does little to lessen the startling impact of Jesus' willingness to identify with ordinary sinners. Matthew, however, includes a short dialogue between John and Jesus in which John protests that he has no right to baptize Jesus. Jesus' reply, while offering no explanation, assures John—and the reader—that the baptism is necessary: "Let it be so now," he tells John, "for thus it is fitting for us to fulfill all righteousness" (Matt. 3:15).

Luke includes no such dialogue in recounting the story of Jesus' baptism—in fact, he does not mention John by name as the baptizer—and he places the incident of John's imprisonment (3:19–20) before Jesus' baptism (3:21–22). John's role is strictly preparatory. As soon as Jesus takes the stage, John makes his exit, and his only subsequent appearance (7:18–35) is as a witness to Jesus.

There is good reason to believe that the story of Jesus' baptism by John is based on historical fact. We are given little information about the actual event, however. We are not privy to Jesus' thoughts about his baptism; we read nothing about psychological preparation. Novelists' delight in using the story to mark the dawning of Jesus' consciousness of his messianic role arises from their own imagination. The story is important to Luke, not for the light it sheds on Jesus' self-understanding, not even for its impact on John or the crowds. The scene is significant because it provides the reader with important information about Jesus, information intelligible only to those familiar with Jewish tradition, however.

The key to the interpretation of the scene is found in the words spoken from heaven: "Thou art my beloved Son; with thee I am well pleased." At least two scriptural passages appear to lie behind the divine pronouncement. The first is Isaiah 42:1:

> Behold my servant, whom I uphold,
>   my chosen, in whom my soul delights;
> I have put my Spirit upon him,
>   he will bring forth justice to the nations.

Selection by the Spirit is a familiar theme in stories about the call of prophets. In Luke, the servant is not simply a prophet. His identity is clarified by another scriptural image, this time from Psalm 2:7:

> I will tell of the decree of the LORD;
> He said to me, "You are my son,
>   today I have begotten you."

The line from the psalm, which was an ancient coronation ritual, is now pronounced by God at Jesus' baptism. The psalm speaks of the king as God's "anointed" (Messiah, in Hebrew; Christ, in Greek). In this scene, God testifies that Jesus is the expected King, and the coming of the Spirit upon Jesus is interpreted as his "anointing" for office. The formal inauguration of Jesus' career at the synagogue in Nazareth (Luke 4:16–30) draws on this imagery. By means of traditional scriptural imagery, Jesus' baptism is interpreted as his anointing.

A final stage in Jesus' preparation is required before he begins his ministry. He must undergo a period of testing in the desert, much like Moses. In his lonely combat with Satan, Jesus rejects crude display of miracles and sheer political force as means to his goal (Luke 4:1–13). He demonstrates here his mastery over Satan, a mastery reflected in his own exorcisms and in those of his followers. The ominous conclusion of the temptation story indicates, however, that the confrontation is not yet over: "And when the devil had ended every temptation, he departed from him until an opportune time" (Luke 4:13). On this disquieting note Jesus opens his public ministry.

Luke chooses not to begin his narrative at the beginning. In his Gospel the formal commencement of Jesus' career is set in a synagogue at Nazareth, a scene for which Jesus' reputation as a teacher and healer is a necessary presupposition. The carefully crafted scene offers a preliminary interpretation of Jesus' career and intimates what is to come. Mark begins with an exorcism; Matthew opens Jesus' ministry with the Sermon on the Mount. Luke chooses to begin with Jesus' appearance in his home town.

Inauguration: Preaching at Nazareth
(Luke 4:16–30; parallels in Mark 6:1–6 and Matt. 13:53–58)

The scene easily divides into two parts. In the first (Luke 4:16–22a), Jesus' role is limited to standing, opening, reading, and offering a single comment on the biblical passage: "Today this scripture has been fulfilled in your hearing" (Luke 4:21). In the second (Luke 4:22b–30), Jesus plays a more aggressive role, taking up an implied challenge by the crowd. He offers a more extended comment on the passage from Isaiah, drawing material from other biblical passages (1 and 2 Kings). In part one, the crowd seems impressed and favorably disposed toward Jesus; in part two, the crowd reacts violently to Jesus' message, seeking to throw him off a cliff at the edge of town. Our task is to understand how the two parts of the scene relate to each other and how the scene as a whole serves to introduce Jesus' ministry in Luke.[1]

The scriptural passage read by Jesus provides the focal point of the story. The passage is from Isaiah:

> The Spirit of the Lord GOD is upon me
>   because the LORD has anointed me
> to bring good tidings to the afflicted;
>   he has sent me to bind up the brokenhearted,
> to proclaim liberty to the captives,
>   and the opening of the prison to those who are bound;
> to proclaim the year of the LORD's favor. . . . (Isa. 61:1–2a)

There is a slight modification of the quotation in Luke, apparently including a line from Isaiah 58:6 ("to set at liberty those who are oppressed").

In Isaiah 61, the prophet announces the dawning of a long-awaited day, the arrival of the jubilee year (see Lev. 25:10), the "acceptable year of the LORD," a time when debts would be cancelled and Jews returned to their ancestral lands. The prophetic message is taken up by Jesus as the theme of his ministry as God's anointed. "Today" marks the fulfillment of the age-old hope. The passage details the career of the one anointed by the Spirit; Jesus will preach principally to the poor and the oppressed. His role will include not only announcing release, however; he will himself set free those in captivity to Satan and his host as well as those bound by illness. The motif appears in Acts as a summary of Jesus' career:

> You know . . . how God anointed Jesus of Nazareth with the Holy Spirit and with power; how he went about doing good and healing all that were oppressed by the devil, for God was with him. (Acts 10:36–38)

Themes take life in stories about Jesus. In the ensuing narrative he eats with "sinners and tax collectors," heals the sick, casts out demons, even raises the dead. When John the Baptist sends messengers from his cell to ask whether Jesus actually is the one whose coming has been awaited (Luke 7:20), Jesus responds:

> Go and tell John what you have seen and heard: the blind receive their sight, the lame walk, lepers are cleansed, and the deaf hear, the dead are raised up, and the poor have the good news preached to them. And blessed is he who takes no offense at me. (Luke 7:22–23)

Jesus' message to John makes explicit what the narrative implies: the words of Isaiah indeed find their fulfillment in the career of this one who has been anointed by the Spirit of God. Jesus' career is in accordance with the Scriptures.

Jesus' suggestion that some might take offense at him picks up another familiar theme. His career will not be one of unbounded success. By the end of the opening scene at the synagogue in Nazareth, Jesus' audience is ready to kill him. There may even be a hint of such conflict in the biblical quotation. The line from Isaiah 58, for example, is lifted from an oracle announcing judgment on Israel for preferring religious ceremony to true obedience to the law, interpreted as concern for the poor and the oppressed (Isa. 58:6–7). It is perhaps overly subtle to argue that one line from Isaiah 58 could serve as a reminder of the whole oracle, but the parallel between the careers of Isaiah and Jesus is difficult to miss. Jesus' career is scriptural not only because he preaches and heals; it embodies tensions common to the experience of Israel's prophets. Like most of God's messengers, Jesus will encounter opposition. His career, as Simeon predicted, is set "for the fall and rising of many within Israel"; he will be a "sign that is spoken against" (Luke 2:34).

The comments of the crowd in Luke 4:22 provide a transition from the first half of the scene to the second. The initial reaction of the worshipers gathered at the synagogue seems positive. The translation of the verse in the NEB, however, may more aptly capture the sense of the Greek, which suggests puzzlement as well as admiration:

> There was a general stir of admiration; they were surprised that words of such grace should fall from his lips. "Is this not Joseph's son?" they asked.

The friendly tone changes abruptly with Jesus' response: "Doubtless you will quote to me. . . . Truly, I say to you. . . . " He appears to read a challenge in the crowd's reaction to him that at least on the surface seemed positive: is the problem the crowd's surprise that Jesus should speak so well? or is it their belief that he is the son of Joseph? or is Jesus aware of unstated misgivings? The author offers little help in answering our questions. We are not told why Jesus should expect hostility, though Simeon has already predicted it. As the scene continues, however, we become increasingly aware that Jesus' expectations are justified. Hostility lies just beneath the surface.

Jesus' reputation as a healer has preceded him to his home town. He anticipates that his neighbors will challenge that reputation; however he does not offer to impress them with miracles. Quoting an old maxim, he predicts that he will find little respect among his own people. Rather than performing signs, he refers them to two of Israel's most famous prophets, Elijah and Elisha. These prophets were sent to "foreigners" (Luke 4:25–27). Those familiar with the biblical sagas would know that both prophets received a hostile reception from their own people, particularly Elijah, who was forced to flee for his life. Jesus' appeal to stories from 1 and 2 Kings provides an interpretation of the earlier citation from Isaiah. Jesus is indeed, like the ancient prophets, the one God has anointed to bring good news to the poor and to deliver captives from bondage. His mission, however, will not be restricted to the "elect." Like

Elijah and Elisha, Jesus will be sent to outsiders, to sinners and tax collectors. Eventually even Gentiles will come to share in Israel's blessings. And like those prophets of old, Jesus will encounter opposition from within the family. Hostility can be expected; it is even "necessary," a term Luke uses frequently. The crisis Jesus will precipitate within Jewish society will be a major theme in the ensuing narrative. "The thoughts of many hearts will be revealed," as Simeon predicted.

Some care is necessary here. Luke has traditionally been viewed as the evangelist with the most universalistic outlook, who tells how the gospel reached beyond the Jewish community to the Gentiles. That is certainly a basic theme of his narrative, especially pronounced in Acts. That need not imply, however, that the Christian message is torn from its Jewish roots or that Gentiles are saved at the expense of Israel. Jesus does anticipate here that "foreigners" will share in Israel's blessings. He does not say that Israel will be replaced by a "new Israel" composed of Gentile Christians. No reference is made anywhere in Luke-Acts to a wholesale rejection of Israel. Israel remains God's elect; thousands of Jews, even in Jerusalem, will believe the gospel (Acts 2; 3; 4; 21:20). There will be opposition to Jesus and his followers from within Israel, as the opening scene demonstrates, but Jesus' career is located squarely within the tradition of Israel's prophets. Even opposition has precedent, and some within Israel will understand.

Despite the preparation, the violence of the crowd's reaction is shocking. The vehemence of their opposition to the notion that God's grace should be given primarily to outsiders reveals that Jesus has touched a sensitive nerve. Lines are drawn. The division within Israel, predicted by Simeon, has begun. Though Jesus manages to escape death here, we cannot but wonder what will happen later—whether the devil will find an "opportune time," or whether his enemies will eventually do him in. We are prepared for the hostility directed at Jesus later. We are also prepared for the heated controversy that arises over the question of admission of Gentiles in Acts (Acts 10; 11; and 15). And we will not be surprised by the violence encountered by such nonconformists as Stephen and Paul. Though we do not yet fully understand the crowd's hostility, we are properly introduced to a story in which conflict and division will be dominant motifs.

The opening scene in the synagogue at Nazareth thus provides a framework within which Jesus' career is to be located. As God's anointed, he will preach, battle the devil, heal the sick, and display particular concern for the poor. He will also generate controversy and, eventually, be killed. This framework is not to be understood solely in terms of its literary function. It is derived from the Scriptures. The events which occur are not isolated or accidental; they are "necessary," part of a plan which the author traces back to the mind of God.

The Herald of Good News

One of the tasks assigned Jesus as the Lord's anointed is to announce good news to the poor. Appropriately, a large portion of Luke's Gospel is devoted to Jesus' teaching. The rubric "heralding good news to the poor" is a bit restrictive, however. Jesus' teachings fall into a variety of groupings, one of which could be described as instructions on discipleship. Jesus teaches his followers how to pray, talks about faith, and offers advice about how to face coming adversities. Another grouping focuses on controversy. Jesus responds to criticism by telling parables or by making pronouncements about sensitive matters or, in some cases, by delivering scathing indictments of his opponents. Still another way to group his sayings would be to focus on those dealing with wealth, a concern throughout Luke's Gospel. Jesus talks frequently about the dangers of wealth as well as its possibilities, about those who know how to use money and those who do not.

Most students of the New Testament choose to group teachings under formal headings.[2] Decades ago, biblical scholars noticed that Jesus' sayings could be separated into categories relating to discernible patterns. One category might be called "controversy stories." Jesus' controversies with his adversaries seem to follow regular patterns; several occur in Luke 5—6. Each episode begins with a general setting: "And Levi made him a great feast in his house; and there was a large company of tax collectors and others sitting at table with them" (Luke 5:29); "On a sabbath, while he was going through the grainfields . . . " (Luke 6:1); "On another sabbath, when he entered the synagogue and taught . . . " (Luke 6:6). The controversy is introduced by opponents, usually Pharisees, who criticize Jesus' behavior:

> And the Pharisees and their scribes murmured against his disciples, saying, "Why do you eat and drink with tax collectors and sinners?" (Luke 5:30)

> And they said to him, "The disciples of John fast often and offer prayers, and so do the disciples of the Pharisees, but yours eat and drink." (Luke 5:33)

> But some of the Pharisees said, "Why are you doing what is not lawful to do on the sabbath?" (Luke 6:2)

Each little scene concludes with a statement of Jesus that settles the dispute, such as, "Those who are well have no need of a physician but those who are sick; I have not come to call the righteous, but sinners to repentance" (Luke 5:31–32). The lack of interest in follow-up—i.e., the response of the disciples or of Jesus' critics—suggests that the little stories were told to feature a pronouncement of Jesus about an important matter. The form of the story corresponds to its function.

Scholars have identified other forms, as in parables or predictions of the future. Study of the formal characteristics of the gospel tradition led many to argue that stories about Jesus and accounts of his teaching had undergone a period of oral transmission prior to their incorporation into written Gospels. "Form critics," as they came to be known, trained in the study of folklore, argued that the forms served as convenient carriers for tales and sayings, reflecting both the need to cast the material into easily-remembered units as well as the purpose the stories served within the church. Martin Dibelius, one of the most famous form critics, insisted that the evangelists should be viewed less as authors than as collectors of tradition.[3] Even form critics recognized, however, that the Gospel writers were responsible for selecting teachings and placing them into some larger framework. Jesus' teachings may thus be studied as separate units, with attention to formal characteristics, and as pieces of a larger whole. Form critics were interested in the former, while more recent scholarship has tended to focus on the latter.[4]

Probably the most familiar form within the corpus of Jesus' teaching is the parable. Luke includes no less than twenty-nine, among them some of the best-known stories in the New Testament, like the parable of the Good Samaritan and of the Prodigal Son. An immense literature has developed around the parables during this century, generated in large measure by the work of a German scholar named Adolph Jülicher.[5]

Writing around the turn of the century, Jülicher broke with centuries of Christian interpretive tradition when he insisted that the parables should be read not as allegories but as one-point stories. Since the time of the church's beginnings, parables had been interpreted as allegories; interpreters identified each feature of the parable as having a particular referent. Jülicher insisted that parables were not to be read in such fashion. An allegory, he insisted, is a cryptogram that demands to be deciphered; it is a story whose only significance is the detailed comparison with something else. The elaborate visions of beasts in the Apocalypse of John are allegories. The images have no significance in themselves; some cannot even be pictured in the mind. Each detail of the beast represents something else. The beast seated on seven hills obviously represents Rome; the crowned ten heads of the beast represent a succession of kings.

New Testament parables are very different from such bizarre and mysterious images. There is nothing cryptic about Jesus' little stories. The longer stories could have happened; perhaps some are drawn from actual experience. It is quite conceivable that a despised Samaritan stopped to assist an injured man on the infamous road from Jerusalem to Jericho, or that a profligate son returned home to rejoin his family. Stories about farmers or about small seeds that grow into large bushes arise directly from life in rural Palestine. If some of Jesus' parables came to be read as allegories even within the New Testament (e.g., the Parable of the Sower in Luke 8:4–15), the reason should be sought within the experience of believers who remembered the stories and handed them on. When Jesus' parables, intended for a specific audience and to make a particular point, were told in new settings, they either took on new meanings or had to be reinterpreted.

Following the lead of Jülicher, scholars like C. H. Dodd[6] and J. Jeremias[7] examined the parables in order to recover their original meanings. They noted that in their use of the stories, Christian interpreters had sometimes added new punchlines or had supplied a new setting that decisively altered the meaning. The parable of the shepherd who leaves the ninety-nine sheep to find the one that is lost, told in Luke in response to criticisms that Jesus associates with the wrong sort of people (Luke 15:3–7), becomes in Matthew an illustration of the ends to which believers should go to bring back errant members of the family (Matt. 18:12–14). Still other students of parables, as R. Funk,[8] have devoted themselves to studying parables as forms of communication, exploring how the stories work and what impact they have on an audience.

Another way to study parables—and of more significance for our task—is to examine their function in the story. Whatever their prehistory or their place in earlier tradition, parables have an important place in Luke. Several focus on matters of possessions and their use. Such parables include:

The Two Debtors	Luke	7:41–43
The Good Samaritan		10:29–37
The Rich Fool		12:16–21
The Unjust Steward		16:1–8
The Rich Man and Lazarus		16:19–31
The Parable of the Pounds		19:11–27

All but one of these stories are unique to Luke. The narrator is obviously interested in the problems and possibilities of possessions. In her *Magnificat,* Mary praises God as the one who fills the hungry with good things and sends the rich empty away. Jesus offers illustrations: the problem is not possessions as such, but the failure to use them properly. Those who do not use even what little they have, like the pathetic servant who hid the money he was given by his master (Luke 19:20–27), are as blameworthy as those who use what they have for selfish purposes, without thought for others—like the rich fool or the rich man who did nothing to aid the beggar outside his gates. The rich man goes to Hades because he refused alms for the needy—while Lazarus goes to Abraham's bosom simply because he was poor. The reversals promised early in the story are stark: it is easier for a camel to pass through the eye of a needle than for the rich to enter the kingdom of God (Luke 18:24–25).

Wealth is of such concern because it is tied to fundamental religious matters. The chasms that separate rich and poor, weak and powerful, insider and outsider, are not intended by God. Possessions are to be used to elevate the downtrodden and to feed the hungry. As in Israel's prophetic tradition, true piety consists in caring for the helpless, the "fatherless and the widow." Charity constitutes true faithfulness to the Torah.

The story of the Good Samaritan illustrates the point. When asked by a lawyer what God expects of the elect, Jesus answers in traditional form: love God and your neighbor (Luke 10:25–28). "And who is my neighbor?" (Luke 10:29) the lawyer asks. Abstractions are of little use; commandments must become specific and concrete. Thus Jesus provides an example of piety. He tells the story of a man in desperate need of help, a victim left for dead along the road. The two characters in the little drama who refuse to help are religious functionaries. If the man were dead, touching him would render them unclean, unable to perform their religious duties. They refuse to give help, not because of indifference, but out of a sense of obligation to their tradition. Ritual purity is uppermost in their minds.

The Samaritan, with no pretense about ritual purity, offers help. His display of generosity is what makes him the "neighbor"—and what stamps him as the truly religious man who fulfills the law. The pious are not the priest and the Levite, not the Pharisees preoccupied with their purity, but those who learn to give, like Zacchaeus, the infamous tax collector who gives half of his possessions away (Luke 19:1–10). Though the theme is not as prominent in Acts, the narrator still takes pains to describe the major figures in the new movement as almsgivers. Sharing of possessions and aid for the poor will characterize the first congregation in Jerusalem (Acts 2:44–45; 4:32–37).

The story of the merciful Samaritan highlights another theme prominent in Jesus' teaching and ministry: the attack on exclusivism. The hero of the parable is not a strict Jew, but a Samaritan, a half-Jew despised by Israelites. It is hardly accidental that in Jesus' story of the Pharisee and the tax collector (Luke 18:9–14), the model of piety is the tax collector, a hated agent of Roman occupation forces noted for dishonesty.

Jesus' teaching is not separated from his deeds. He lives what he preaches. Several of his stories are told in response to criticism leveled by religious detractors. Jesus is consistently attacked for associating with "sinners and tax collectors." Most problematic of all, Jesus eats with them. Meals were of particular significance to Easterners. They offered a rare opportunity for intimacy. Serious Jews recognized the potential of intimacy as a religious force and sought reinforcement of their religious concerns by eating together. Special groups were singled out as table fellowships. Meals served to reinforce traditional religious concerns. Pharisees, rigorous Jews who believed that a true Israelite ought to be pure at all times and not just at worship, testified to their faith by eating only with others who respected purity laws and paid the taxes on food stipulated in the law. In a world increasingly fragmented, table fellowship offered a visible sign of Jewish identity and a concrete reminder of the power of tradition to order life. As the song says in *Fiddler on the Roof*, the community survives by tradition.

Serious Jews were thus troubled by Jesus' behavior. He was obviously religious himself, otherwise he could have been written off as a heretic or a pagan. Though concerned about tradition, however, he refused to respect boundaries. From the outset he associated with outcasts, people whose lives seemed to demonstrate contempt for traditional piety. In the eyes of his contemporaries he risked contamination by associating with the impious, and his actions threatened the carefully monitored structure that guaranteed a place for Judaism in the world.

Why does Jesus eat with sinners and tax collectors? The question runs throughout the story. The reason is not, Jesus insists, that he has no interest in tradition or that he is indifferent about behavior. His behavior may be compared with that of a shepherd who leaves the whole flock just to seek one sheep that is lost. It is like that of a woman who loses one coin and leaves everything until she has found it. There is something extravagant, almost careless, about Jesus' singleminded interest in the lost. That is the way God is, Jesus insists. God is concerned with repentance, interested in lives that can be turned around—about brothers and sisters who can be brought back into the family. Bringing back the lost is worth any risk.

To defend his actions, Jesus tells the story of the Prodigal Son—or, as some have suggested, the story of the Waiting Father. In the familiar parable, a restive son, eager to gain his freedom and to see the world, requests his inheritance. Such a request was perfectly legitimate in Jewish society. His subsequent behavior was not. The things on which he squanders his money could only elicit contempt from those serious about piety. In fact, the youth lacks any sense at all. In the end, he loses everything: the young Jew is reduced to feeding pigs, unclean animals. When in absolute desperation he "comes to himself" and returns home, he is utterly astonished to find a father eager to welcome him back into the family.

As in other two-part parables, the emphasis falls on the second half of the story. In the concluding scene, the older brother confronts his father with the gross injustice he has suffered. Not surprisingly, he resents the attention paid to the young profligate. The father's actions seem to condone wastefulness and irresponsibility.

> "Lo, these many years I have served you, and I never disobeyed your command; yet you never gave me a kid, that I might make merry with my friends. But when this son of *yours* [emphasis added] came, who has devoured your living with harlots, you killed for him the fatted calf!" (Luke 15:29–30)

The father's poignant response with which the parable ends serves as Jesus' counter-question to his critics:

> "Son, you are always with me, and all that is mine is yours. It was fitting to make merry and be glad, for this *your* [emphasis added] brother was dead, and is alive; he was lost, and is found." (Luke 15:31–32)

He is "your" brother, the father tells his son. The older brother views him as an outsider, as someone to whom he is not related ("this son of yours"). The real problem is the older brother's. Though he appropriately despises the life his brother has lived, he is unable to recognize that they are brothers. If he could understand that, he would be able to share his father's joy. The younger son has learned his lesson and is ready to live a useful life. The older brother has learned nothing; he cannot see beyond his rights. For him, the family has become exclusive, a means of keeping others out. Like the allegedly pious Jews, he is in need of conversion. He lacks desperately the love God displays in welcoming back strays. He has no sense of what it really means to be a neighbor.

Jesus' ministry and his teachings embody God's concern for sinners. God is not indifferent. The law is to be obeyed, but religion that becomes merely exclusive, that seeks to perpetuate social injustice, that destroys any genuine concern for outsiders, is perverse. The pious in Luke fear contamination from outsiders. Jesus is not corrupted, however. By their contact with him, sinners and tax collectors—people like Matthew and Zacchaeus—are converted, reformed, restored. Touching the woman with a hemorrhage (Luke 8:43–48) or lepers (Luke 5:12–15 and 17:11–19) or even the dead (Luke 7:11–17) does not defile Jesus; rather, the sick are healed, lepers cleansed, and the dead raised.

Revolutionary forces are at work in Jesus' ministry. He does not leave the world as he finds it. Tensions exist between Jesus' teachings and traditional ways of being religious. He attacks custom and precedent, and his ministry will have social and political implications. There will be reversals. However, the point is not that Jesus came to destroy the law; he did not set out to destroy Judaism. His teaching about outcasts and his attack on false piety and exclusivism, just as his instruction about wealth, are firmly anchored in the prophetic tradition. If he meets opposition, it is because others do not properly understand the will of God. The thoughts of many hearts are revealed. Many will fall because of Jesus, but it is for a greater good. Jesus seeks to gather the faithful, to bring the errant back into the fold, to enlist his followers in making piety the positive force it was intended to be. "Be merciful," Jesus exhorts, "even as your Father is merciful" (Luke 6:36).

The Deliverer

As Savior, Jesus is not only herald of the "acceptable year of the LORD" about to dawn; he is primarily its agent. His healings and exorcisms are central to his role as the Lord's anointed. In Acts, his deeds are essential to the message preached by his followers:

> "Jesus of Nazareth, a man attested to you by God with mighty works and wonders and signs which God did though him in your midst. . . . (Acts 2:22)

> "You know . . . how God anointed Jesus of Nazareth with the Holy Spirit and with power; how he went about doing good and healing all that were oppressed by the devil. . . . " (Acts 10:36–38)

Though stories of Jesus' miracles and his struggles with demons are less prominent in Luke than in Mark, acts of deliverance are a significant feature of his career. Jesus heals the sick, casts out demons, even raises the dead.

As with Jesus' teachings, stories about healings and exorcisms seem to follow certain patterns. Though it is somewhat difficult to speak of specific "forms" of stories employing rigid categories, there are certain family similarities among various types. In some narratives, the faith of those healed is central. In chapter 5, there are two stories in which faith is rewarded. In Luke 5:12–15, a leper comes to Jesus begging for help, confident that Jesus can cure his disease. His confidence is rewarded. In the subsequent episode (vss. 17–26), a group of men bring a paralyzed friend to Jesus. They are so confident Jesus can help that when they are unable to get through the crowd they remove part of the roof to get their friend into the room. This particular story is complicated, since it also includes a controversy between Jesus and the religious authorities, but it does highlight the importance of faith. Like the centurion who asks Jesus' help (Luke 7:1–10), Jairus (Luke 8:40–42), or the woman with a hemorrhage (Luke 8:43–48), the friends of the paralytic discover the rewards of faith in Jesus the deliverer. One can almost hear the preacher in the background exhorting his audience to have such faith.

Other stories have little to do with faith. The exorcisms typically focus not on the faith of the one healed, since those under the power of demons have no will of their own. The demoniacs in the synagogue at Capernaum (Luke 4:31–37) and the demoniac in the land of the Gerasenes (Luke 8:26–39) have no control over themselves. Dialogue is between Jesus and the demons. The stories, told with a relish for detail, focus exclusively on the power of the exorcist. They are told to elicit awe and amazement. Such stories have parallels in other ancient literature. The detailed description of maladies, comments about the reaction of the crowds, and proofs that a cure had been effected are all accepted elements of this narrative genre. Form critics seek to distinguish such stories from those that highlight the power of faith.

An interesting example of this latter type of miracle story from non-Christian literature, in this case from Philostratus' *Life of Apollonius*,[9] highlights both what Luke shares with other ancient authors and what distinguishes his work.

> Here also is a miracle *(thauma)* of Apollonius. A young girl seemed to have died in the very hour of her marriage and the bridegroom was following the bier weeping over his unfulfilled marriage. Rome mourned also, for it happened that the dead girl was from one of the best families. Apollonius, happening to be present where they were mourning, said, "Put down the bier, for I will end your weeping for this girl," and at the same time he asked what her name was. The bystanders thought that he was going to give a speech like those which people give at burials to heighten everyone's sorrow. But he didn't; instead he touched her and saying something no one could hear, awakened the girl who seemed dead. And the girl spoke and went back to her father's house, just like Alcestis who was brought back to her life by Herakles. And when the relatives of the girl offered Apollonius 150,000 silver pieces as a reward, he replied that he would return it to the child as a gift for her dowry.
>
> Now whether he found a spark of life in her which had escaped the notice of the doctors—for it is said her breath could be seen above her face as it rained—or whether, her life actually being completely extinguished, she grew warm again and received it back, no one knows. A grasp of this mystery has not been gained either by me or by those who chanced to be there. (*Life of Apollonius of Tyana* IV, 45ff.)[10]

The story is remarkably similar to one told about Jesus.

> Soon afterward he went to a city called Nain, and his disciples
> and a great crowd went with him. As he drew near to the gate of the
> city, behold, a man who had died was being carried out, the only son
> of his mother, and she was a widow; and a large crowd from the city
> was with her. And when the Lord saw her, he had compassion on her
> and said to her, "Do not weep." And he came and touched the bier,
> and the bearers stood still. And he said, "Young man, I say to you,
> arise." And the dead man sat up, and began to speak. And he gave
> him to his mother. Fear seized them all; and they glorified God,
> saying, "A great prophet has arisen among us!" and "God has
> visited his people!" And this report concerning him spread through
> the whole of Judea and all the surrounding country. (Luke 7:11–17)

The similarities are striking. In both accounts, the wonder-
worker encounters a funeral procession already in progress. The
situation seems hopeless. The unexpected intervention by the hero,
the miracle and proof (the dead speak), and the reaction of the
crowd, seem to follow a pattern. The story seeks to elicit from the
reader a reaction similar to that of the crowd.

The differences are equally striking. Philostratus, the biographer of Apollonius, was a man of letters. He wrote, as did his
contemporaries, about important people and events. Kings,
generals, highly placed officials, and philosophers were fit subjects
for biographies. Common people were of interest only as comic
relief. In Philostratus' story, the pathos evoked is appropriate to his
audience's social class. The woman who had died was about to be
married. The grieving bridegroom had been deprived of his bride.
The crowd of mourners ("Rome") testifies to the social status of the
young woman. Her return to life elicits an apt response: her parents
seek to make Apollonius a rich man—which he appropriately
refuses, since he is an ascetic.

The scene in Luke is characteristically different. From the
outset, Jesus has cast his lot with the lower classes—with shepherds,
country priests, harlots, and the unemployed. The funeral he
interrupts is for a young man whose mother is a widow. She has been
deprived not only of her husband and her son, but also of her only
means of support. The pathos is appropriate to those with little

money and few prospects. Jesus' restoration of the young man to life not only reunites the family but guarantees that the woman will be able to live.

There are also differences in the narrators' reaction to the miraculous. Philostratus is a rationalist. He doubts that a miracle really occurred and allows his doubt to color the story. His hero Apollonius is more a sage than a wonder-worker. Luke and his audience, however, have no doubts about Jesus' ability to raise the dead. The perspective is not that of an aristocratic, detached observer; it is that of one who knows life to be a battle between the forces of evil and the forces of good and who does not doubt for a moment the possibility of miraculous deliverance any less than the reality of bondage to evil.

There is one final difference between the two accounts that accentuates an important aspect of the Gospel narrative. To make sense of the miracle, Philostratus and his audience refer to classical mythology. The resurrection of the young girl is like that of Alcestis; Apollonius may be compared to Herakles. In Luke's Gospel, the framework is biblical. Those who witness the miracle praise God and express their conviction that Jesus is a great prophet. Jesus' miracles can be understood only within the larger framework Luke and his tradition provide.

The author fashions the framework largely from Israel's dreams and hopes. For decades, perhaps centuries, Jews had longed for the dawning of God's rule over the world, the kingdom of God. However expectations differed, all hoped for God's intervention and for deliverance from bondage and oppression. According to Luke, Jesus' career marks the dawning of that kingdom. In an episode recounted in chapter 11, Jesus is accused by religious leaders of being in league with the prince of demons. Religious leaders do not dispute his power. They insist, however, that it derives not from God but from the devil. Jesus' response not only emphasizes the absurdity of their claim but offers his own estimate of the significance of exorcisms:

> "For you say that I cast out demons by Beelzebul. And if I cast out demons by Beelzebul, by whom do your sons cast them out? Therefore they shall be your judges. But if it is by the finger of God

that I cast out demons, then the kingdom of God has come upon you. When a strong man, fully armed, guards his own palace, his goods are in peace; but when one stronger than he assails him and overcomes him, he takes away his armor, in which he trusted, and divides his spoil." (Luke 11:18–22)

Jesus is the one stronger than Satan, come to set captives free by invading the stronghold of the evil one. Satan boasted earlier in the Gospel (Luke 4:5–7) that all the kingdoms of the world belonged to him. Jesus contests that mastery, and his exorcisms offer evidence of his success. They represent the dawning of a new day: the kingdom of God has come you. Jesus is not simply herald of the kingdom; he is the agent of its inauguration.

In his role as the agent of the kingdom, Jesus also fulfills prophecies. His deeds evidence his concern for those in bondage to sin and the power of evil and reveal his power, but they also point back to the biblical framework within which Israel pictured the future. In the synagogue at Nazareth, Jesus quotes Isaiah 61, commenting that the prophecy is fulfilled "today." Jesus' words for John the Baptist in Luke 7:22 hark back not only to Isaiah 61 but to other familiar passages, like Isaiah 35:5–6:

> Then the eyes of the blind shall be opened,
>   and the ears of the deaf unstopped;
> then shall the lame man leap like a hart,
>   and the tongue of the dumb sing for joy.

Within the framework of Israel's heritage, Jesus' miracles offer evidence that ancient promises are now being fulfilled. These are not isolated occurrences, but "events that have been fulfilled in our midst" (Luke 1:1, author's translation).

Even more specifically, Jesus' miracles provide testimony that he is one of the prophets (or perhaps *the* prophet) promised in the Scriptures. When Jesus asks his followers what people think of him, they reply, "John the Baptist; but others say, Elijah; and others, that one of the old prophets has risen" (Luke 9:19). When Jesus raised the son of the widow, the crowd responded, "A great prophet has arisen among us!" In the opening scene at the synagogue in Nazareth, Jesus read a quotation associated with activities traditionally linked with prophets. In Jewish tradition, prophets and the Messiah were distinct figures; for believers in Jesus, they merge.

It is not difficult to understand why people might have viewed Jesus as a prophet. Like the prophets of old, he spoke on his own authority ("not like the scribes"). His miracles were reminiscent of the deeds of some of Israel's greatest prophets, Elijah and Elisha. Both Elijah (1 Kings 17:17–24) and Elisha (2 Kings 4:18–37) brought young children back to life. Elisha fed a large number of people with only a few loaves "and had some left" (2 Kings 4:42–44; cf. Luke 9:10–17). Since Elijah's return was predicted (Malachi 4:5–6), it is not surprising that some believed Jesus to be the great prophet come to herald the new day.

Even more crucial are parallels to traditions about Moses from Deuteronomy. A prophet, as defined in Deuteronomy, is one who speaks on God's behalf and performs signs and wonders. Moses serves as the embodiment of that ideal, interpreting God's will to Israel and performing miracles in the wilderness. Even in Deuteronomy, Moses is important not only as a figure from the past but as a prototype:

> "The LORD your God will raise up for you a prophet like me from among you, from your brethren—him you shall heed. . . . And the LORD said to me, 'They have rightly said all that they have spoken. I will raise up for them a prophet like you from among their brethren; and I will put my words in his mouth, and he shall speak to them all that I command him.'" (Deut. 18:15–18)

Some scholars believe the promise originally referred to a succession of prophets, others that it pointed to Elijah. In Jesus' day, however, pious Jews read the passage as an oracle predicting the coming of a prophet at the end of days.[11] In Acts 3, Peter explicitly identifies Jesus as that "prophet like Moses," quoting Deuteronomy 18 (Acts 3:22–26). The identification provides a setting within which to understand Jesus' miracles (prophets perform "signs and wonders") as well as his teaching. The quotation from Deuteronomy also provides Jesus' followers with a crucial piece of information: the true prophet provides a test of Israel's fidelity to God:

> "And whoever will not give heed to my words which he shall speak in my name, I myself will require it of him." (Deut. 18:19)

Those who murmur against Jesus as Israelites once murmured against Moses show themselves to be false Jews. Peter draws the inevitable conclusion: those who do not heed Jesus and his words will be "destroyed from the people" (Acts 3:23).

That same prophetic tradition sheds light on the complexity of the problem faced by Israel's rulers. It is not only true prophets who perform "signs and wonders," as Deuteronomy 13 warns:

> If a prophet arises among you, or a dreamer of dreams, and gives you a sign or a wonder, and the sign or the wonder which he tells you comes to pass, and if he says, "Let us go after other gods," which you have not known, "and let us serve them," you shall not listen to the words of that prophet or to that dreamer of dreams; for the LORD your God is testing you. . . . But that prophet or that dreamer of dreams shall be put to death. . . . (Deut. 13:1–5)

Israel's leaders face a difficult task. They must distinguish between true and false prophets. False prophets are to be executed, true prophets heeded. The stakes are high. Jesus' "signs and wonders" cannot be ignored for they identify him as an inspired prophet. The question is by what he is inspired. Is he in league with the devil, as some of his opponents suggest? Does he intend to destroy the temple and change the customs delivered by Moses, as others allege (Acts 6:14)? His lack of concern for traditional forms of piety may mean that he is a false prophet, performing miracles to seduce the populace. If so, Israel's leaders are obliged to silence him. If Jesus is the true prophet, however; if his healings and exorcisms reveal him as God's emissary and the agent of the kingdom; if Jesus is the real prophet like Moses whom God has raised up, Israel is obliged to heed his words. If they refuse, they can no longer lay claim to their heritage; they will be destroyed from the people.

In the eyes of Luke and those for whom he wrote, Jesus was

obviously the Christ, the savior of the world, the prophet like Moses God had raised up to herald the coming of the kingdom and to wrest control from Satan. By so doing, they believed, Jesus had fulfilled promises God had made to the people. They were aware, however, of ambiguities. There were many in Jesus' day and in subsequent times unable to see in his career the hand of God. Israel's leaders had believed Jesus to be little more than a troublemaker with no respect for the tradition. He had power; no one could deny that. But the ancient world could boast other miracle-workers and other religious propagandists. People had to decide in Jesus' case, as in others, what that power meant. Was Jesus God's anointed, come to set the captives free? Or was he only a pretender, a false prophet, a friend of sinners and tax collectors intent upon tearing down the tradition? The fateful question runs through the Gospel and Acts and provides drama to the very end (Acts 28).

King of the Jews

Though the mighty take no note of Jesus' birth, we know they will not be able to ignore for long the one destined to sit on "the throne of his father David" and "reign over the house of Jacob for ever" (Luke 1:32–33). Any compromise with established powers is ruled out in Jesus' initial confrontation with Satan, to whom belong "all the kingdoms of the world" (Luke 4:5). Jesus insures conflict by his refusal of Satan's offer of worldly authority (Luke 4:6–8). His exorcisms reveal his intent to assume control himself. Jesus and the powers of darkness are on a collision course. The narrator's comment in Luke 4:13 that the devil departed until an "opportune time" heightens anticipation of that inevitable confrontation.

The hostility Jesus encounters in Nazareth suggests that perhaps Satan's dominion extends to the leaders in Israel as well. Though Luke does not explicitly characterize Jewish leaders as "children of darkness," as is the case in the Gospel of John, the most important conflicts in the Gospel and in Acts involve leaders of the religious institutions. Struggles with local leaders foreshadow the final conflict with the scribes, the chief priests, and the elders, the group comprising the temple leadership and the official legal authority for the religious community. The highest authorities will have to deal with Jesus, as he predicts:

> "The Son of man must suffer many things, and be rejected by the elders and chief priests and scribes, and be killed, and on the third day be raised." (Luke 9:22)

Ominous rumblings from the storm that will burst in Jerusalem can be heard through the story. There is explicit foreshadowing (Luke 9:44 and 18:31–33) and more subtle anticipation. Most of Jesus' ministry is played out in the shadow of the impending disaster:

> When the days drew near for him to be received up, he set his face to go to Jerusalem. (Luke 9:51)

There is something artificial about the "journey" portion of Luke's Gospel (Luke 9:51—19:27). Though Jesus has allegedly decided that the time has come to make the journey (see also Luke 13:22), little else suggests geographical movement. Episodes are furnished with general settings: "He was praying in a certain place" (Luke 11:1); "Now when he was casting out a demon that was dumb" (Luke 11:14); "When the crowds were increasing" (Luke 11:29); "While he was speaking, a Pharisee asked him to dine with him" (Luke 11:37). As noted earlier, such units bear the earmarks of oral tradition. The so-called "travel narrative" in Luke's Gospel seems more like a collection of various stories and sayings than an actual account of a journey. The author seems to have provided his own framework for the traditional material. The very artificiality of that framework, however, offers testimony to its importance. Jesus' public ministry must be understood in light of what is to come in Jerusalem.

We might ask why it is so important that Jesus travel to Jerusalem. One answer is purely historical: that is where Jesus was rejected by Jewish and Roman leaders and hung on a cross. There is obviously more, however. Luke is aware of the importance of Jerusalem in Jewish tradition. It is the holy city, the place God chose for the holy name to dwell (Ps. 132), the place where God's promised deliverance would begin. The author is also aware of less positive traditions in which Jerusalem plays a central role, traditions even more crucial to his story:

> " 'Nevertheless I must go on my way today and tomorrow and the day following; for it cannot be that a prophet should perish away from Jerusalem.' O Jerusalem, Jerusalem, killing the prophets and stoning those who are sent to you! How often I would have gathered your children together as a hen gathers her brood under her wings, and you would not! Behold, your house is forsaken. And I tell you, you will not see me until you say, 'Blessed is he who comes in the name of the Lord!'" (Luke 13:33–35)

The Jerusalem leaders' rejection of Jesus takes on special significance in light of traditions about the rejection of prophets. Though the Old Testament says little about the death of prophets, post-biblical legends developed, some of which we possess in written form.[12] Drawing on such legends, Luke offers in advance an appraisal of Jesus' rejection. Jesus stands with a succession of God's spokespersons who were ill-treated by God's own people. There is even a sense in which Jesus' rejection and death will complete some terrible pattern, bringing an era to an end:

> "Woe to you! for you build the tombs of the prophets whom your fathers killed. So you are witnesses and consent to the deeds of your fathers; for they killed them, and you build their tombs. Therefore also the Wisdom of God said, 'I will send them prophets and apostles, some of whom they will kill and persecute,' that the blood of all the prophets, shed from the foundation of the world, may be required of this generation. . . . Yes, I tell you, it shall be required of this generation." (Luke 11:47–51)

Jesus' prediction that Jerusalem itself will be destroyed, leaving not one stone on another, completes the picture (Luke 21:5–6).

With Jesus' arrival in Jerusalem, there is an abrupt shift in imagery. The confrontation between Jesus and the institutional leaders has to this point been cast in terms from prophetic tradition. Jesus arrives in Jerusalem as a king, however, riding on a donkey, hailed by the crowds. "Blessed is the King who comes in the name of the Lord. Peace in heaven and glory in the highest," they shout, providing an interesting counterpoint to the song of the angelic host at Jesus' birth (Luke 19:38; see 2:13–14). Royal imagery dominates. Jesus is interrogated as a would-be Messiah by both Jewish and Roman officials (Luke 22:67; 23:2, 3). As he hangs on the cross, he is mocked as "the Christ of God" and "King of the Jews." (Luke 23:35, 37). The charge against Jesus is formulated by Pilate: "This is the King of the Jews."

The royal imagery injects a pronounced note of irony into the story. It seems singularly inappropriate. It may well be that Israel's prophets encountered rejection and were even martyred, however, the same was not expected for the Christ. Even if the confrontation has been anticipated in Luke, the actual event is strangely anti-climactic. The promising young man destined to rule Israel seems powerless. When Satan "entered into Judas" (Luke 22:3), Jesus' movement begins to fall apart. The crowd that hailed him as king proves fickle; their hopes are dashed when Jesus fails to throw off the hated Roman rule. Jesus' disciples, so carefully prepared to carry on his ministry, are a bitter disappointment. Judas betrays Jesus. Peter, whose name means "rock," disintegrates, denying him three times. Jesus' movement ends in shambles at the foot of the cross. Jesus, the "Son of the Most High," heir to the throne of David, mighty exorcist and great teacher, is rejected by the leaders of his own people, tried before Pilate, and dies on a cross. The story takes a surprising turn, distinguishing it from ordinary tales of rulers who arise from humble beginnings. Jesus is a king destined to die. He scarcely looks like the expected "shoot from the stump of Jesse" who will "with the breath of his lips . . . slay the wicked" (Isa. 11:1–4).

The story does not end here, of course. There is another stunning reversal that occurs when God raises Jesus from the dead, making of the rejected stone the "head of the corner" (Ps. 118:22, quoted in Luke 20:17 and Acts 4:11). The author does not pass too quickly over the death scene, however, because it provides a glimpse into the character of human life. Foremost is the irony: things are not as they appear. The religious and political leaders live on the level of appearances. They exercise their authority to preserve the tradition and to keep the peace. Believing Jesus to be a threat to tradition and to law and order, they do away with him.

What they do not understand is that Jesus is God's anointed, sent to herald the rule of God and to set captives free. Ironically, they themselves bear witness to the truth; their mockery of Jesus as King testifies to the truth, though they intend their words as taunts. They appropriately perceive Jesus as a threat to their authority. What they do not recognize is that he is a threat because their authority comes from Satan. By their rejection of Jesus, the true ruler, they seal their own fate (Luke 11:47–51). They participate in world-changing events without any notion of what is occurring, without any inkling that Jesus goes "as it has been determined" (Luke 22:22) or that "the Christ must suffer" (Luke 24:26, 46, author's translation). Through Jesus' brutal death, their masks are stripped away and readers are afforded a glimpse of the way the world really is. Things are not what they seem. Jesus, despised and rejected, is the real ruler and the measure of truth; his would-be judges are judged and shown to be frauds, unfit for rule.

There is a difference between Luke and the other Gospels, however. The world he sketches is not as bleak. Appearance and reality are not separated by an unbridgable chasm as they seem to be in John and in Mark. There is irony, but there is also a recognizable nobility in Jesus even at death. In Mark, for example, the tone is almost overwhelmingly tragic. Jesus is a victim, deserted by his friends, rejected and mocked by everyone. His only words from the cross, "My God, my God, why have you forsaken me?" (Mark 15:34) are misunderstood, and with that he dies. By contrast, Jesus plays an active role in Luke's passion narrative. He delivers a brief homily on the way to Golgotha, warning the weeping women to weep for themselves and not for him (Luke 23:28–31). Facing death himself, he is nevertheless able to offer hope to a repentant criminal executed alongside: "Truly, I say to you, today you will be with me in Paradise" (Luke 23:43).[13] His last words are not the desperate cry of abandonment (from Ps. 22), but more triumphant words from another psalm: "Father, into your hands I commit my spirit!" (Luke 23: 46; cf. Ps. 31:5). Though officials are unable to perceive the truth, others can. One of the criminals understands. The centurion confesses, "Certainly this man was innocent!" (Luke 23:47). Even the onlookers recognize that Jesus' death was a mistake:

> And all the multitude who assembled to see the sight, when they saw
> what had taken place, returned home beating their breasts. (Luke
> 23:48)

If truth lies beneath the surface, it does not lie as far beneath for
Luke as for others. Jesus' greatness is not obscured even by his
humiliating death. Even association with common criminals cannot
defile him; the terrible situation only provides another opportunity
for freeing captives. That nobility spills over into the Acts of the
Apostles. Peter, Stephen, and Paul will emulate their master when
faced with danger and death. Luke comes close to depicting Jesus'
death as exemplary, portraying Jesus as a martyr.

Finally, it is important to the author that the story proceeds
according to plan. Jesus' own predictions are fulfilled in Peter's
denial and in Jesus' arrest and execution. Scripture is also fulfilled.
An example of this fulfillment is the story, unique to Luke, of
Pilate's attempt to have Jesus' case transferred to Herod. Historians
are divided with regard to the legal possibility of such transfer of
jurisdiction. The whole scene is also difficult to square with the
portrait of Pilate offered by Philo and Josephus, Luke's contemporaries. They portray him as a brutal administrator with an intense
dislike for Jews who was finally recalled from office for excessive
brutality.[14] Luke's Pilate seems excessively concerned with the fate
of a lower-class Jew and overly anxious to abdicate his legal
responsibilities.

The point of the little episode is explained in Acts. In 4:25–26,
Peter quotes the first verses of Psalm 2:

> "Why did the Gentiles rage,
> and the peoples imagine vain things?
> The kings of the earth set themselves in array,
> and the rulers were gathered together,
> against the Lord and against his Anointed" (Greek: Christ).

He then offers his interpretation:

> "for truly in this city there were gathered together against thy holy
> servant Jesus, whom thou didst anoint, both Herod and Pontius

> Pilate, with the Gentiles and the peoples of Israel, to do whatever thy hand and thy plan had predestined to take place." (Acts 4:27–28)

Herod is "King of Judea" (Luke 1:5); Pilate is a "ruler." This explains the strange comment Luke makes in the passion narrative:

> And Herod and Pilate became friends with each other that very day, for before this they had been at enmity with each other. (Luke 23:12)

Herod and Pilate unite in their opposition to Jesus. Whatever historical basis there may or may not be for the tale, the little episode fits like a piece in a puzzle. It was anticipated, predestined, necessary. Though Jesus is a king like no other, even his death is part of the plan God had formed from the beginning. "Was it not necessary that the Christ should suffer these things and enter into his glory?" Jesus asks (Luke 24:26). Luke assumes that when the facts are in, most will acknowledge that necessity.

"And on the Third Day Rise"

Apart from the birth narratives, the Gospel writers are nowhere at greater variance than when telling the story of Easter. Agreement among the Synoptic Gospels ends with the story of the empty tomb, lending credibility to the argument that Matthew and Luke used Mark as a source. Matthew and Luke agree with one another only when they agree with Mark. The two Gospels diverge with the ending of Mark at 16:8. To some extent such differences should be anticipated. Probably no point in a story is as crucial as its ending, or as characteristic of a particular author.

In all the Gospels, the principal actors in the opening scene on Easter morning are women. Of Jesus' movement, they alone remain; the men are in hiding. Twice Luke has alerted his readers to their importance, mentioning the "women who had followed him from Galilee" (Luke 23:49, 55). Only they know where he has been buried and they alone take measures to provide a decent burial. They buy spices before the Sabbath begins but then must wait until sunrise on the day after the Sabbath before visiting the tomb.

Small differences set Luke's version of their visit to the empty tomb apart. There are two "men" in "dazzling apparel," rather than one young man (Mark) or one angel (Matthew). In Luke, the women are not told to send the disciples to Galilee where Jesus is to meet them. Galilee is mentioned, but only as the place where Jesus predicted all that was to occur in Jerusalem. The women recall Jesus' prediction and do not even need to be told to spread the news. They run to report what they have seen to "the eleven and to all the rest" (Luke 24:9). Their message is greeted with skepticism by the men, still in hiding.

The detail is not lost on the narrator, who from the outset has shown a marked interest in outcasts and "those of low degree." It is appropriate that women, low on the social scale, should be the first evangelists—as appropriate as that Mary, an ordinary girl, should give birth to the Savior of the world and serve as a model of piety. Reversals occur to the very end.

The centerpiece of Luke's resurrection narrative is the story of Jesus' appearance to two travelers on the road to Emmaus. The length of the tale and the detail are notable. The scene is shrouded in mystery. Only one of the travelers is named—Cleopas, a name that appears nowhere else in the New Testament. Who is the second figure? Someone known to the audience? We can only guess. Jesus' appearance invites speculation. He walks and talks with the travelers as an ordinary human being—yet they do not know him. The author offers no explanations, except that "their eyes were kept from recognizing him" (Luke 24:16).

The dialogue between Jesus and the travelers focuses on their apparently disappointed hopes. "But we had hoped that he was the one to redeem Israel," they tell the stranger. Though the matter is not completely closed because of the strange message of the women and the alleged "vision of angels," the travelers have little hope. In response, Jesus offers a lesson in biblical interpretation:

> "O foolish men, and slow of heart to believe all that the prophets have spoken! Was it not necessary that the Christ should suffer these things and enter his glory?" And beginning with Moses and all the prophets, he interpreted to them in all the scriptures the things concerning himself. (Luke 24:25–27)

The travelers still do not perceive that the stranger is Jesus and that he has been speaking of himself. That recognition occurs only at the table to which, reflecting proper hospitality, they have invited the stranger. Though their "hearts burned within them," it was not until Jesus took bread, gave thanks, and broke it that they recognized him. With that, Jesus vanishes.

The table scene is reminiscent of other meals in Luke, particularly the last meal Jesus shared with his followers when he "took bread, gave thanks, broke, and gave it to them" (Luke 22:19). As the travelers report, Jesus was made known to them "in the breaking of the bread" (Luke 24:35). Whether this refers to the eucharist or to simple table fellowship in Christian homes or to a form of both, the words intentionally anticipate the practice of "breaking bread in their homes" reported in Acts 2:46. It is in the intimacy of table fellowship that the presence of Jesus continues among the faithful.

Some unevenness in the narrative is apparent when the two travelers burst in upon the disciples with their news—only to learn that Jesus has already appeared to Simon (Luke 24:33–34). Nowhere in the New Testament is this appearance recounted, though it is frequently mentioned (1 Cor. 15:5 and Mark 16:7). Like the other evangelists, Luke does not even attempt to be complete. Some stories do not need to be told.

Jesus' appearance to the gathered disciples has a polemical edge. It seems calculated to refute claims that Jesus was a *pneuma*, a spirit or ghost. He eats, now not as a sign of intimacy but as proof that he is flesh and bone (though of an unusual sort, since he can still enter locked rooms and vanish from sight). Perhaps the story is directed against some who claimed that the risen Christ was only an angelic being who had inhabited the earthly Jesus.[15]

The final scene is transitional, drawing together threads within the story and anticipating the next act in the drama.[16] Jesus offers another lesson in biblical interpretation, stressing again the scriptural "necessity" of his death and resurrection. In this instance, however, Jesus makes an addition: "what is written" included the ministry of the apostles.

"Thus it is written . . . that repentance and forgiveness of sins should
be preached in his name to all nations, beginning from Jerusalem."
(Luke 24:46–47)

Acts will tell the story of the witnesses, chosen to preach the
message, and it will offer detailed evidence of the scriptural basis
both of Jesus' ministry and of the ministry of his apostles. Such
substantiation is necessary, since some will not believe the witnesses
just as they did not believe Jesus. Jesus' pronouncement about
scriptural "necessity" will be fleshed out in the speeches in Acts.
The matter is crucial to Luke, who promised at the outset to write
about the things "fulfilled in our midst" to show how well founded
the received tradition was. We would not be far wrong to see in this
argument for scriptural necessity one of the major purposes in
writing the two volumes. To be properly understood, Jesus'
story—and the story of his followers—must be understood within
the framework of the biblical story, Israel's story.

Luke's Gospel ends, as it began, in the temple. The story is not
over, however. Jesus' followers have been told to wait for "power
from on high," power necessary for the carrying out of their
commission to bear testimony to all nations. They have been
warned to expect trouble. The blissful picture with which the
Gospel ends cannot last. The mission will eventually move beyond
Jerusalem, where there will not be left one stone on another. But
that takes us on to part two.

CHAPTER III

"To the End of the Earth"

Acts opens on a note of anticipation. "Lord, will you at this time restore the kingdom to Israel?" Jesus' followers ask. Some commentators regard the question as a misunderstanding typical of followers who have not yet made the transition to the new era in which things pertaining to Israel will be left behind. Jesus does not correct such an alleged misunderstanding, however. In response to their query he simply restates his promise that they will receive power when the Holy Spirit comes upon them, enabling them to carry out their commission (Acts 1:8). They do not need to know "when" (Acts 1:7). The promise of the Spirit recalls the prophecy of John the Baptist about a baptism "with the Holy Spirit and with fire" (Luke 3:16; see Acts 1:5), further linking Acts with what has preceded. Jesus' promise also restates his last words reported in the Gospel (Luke 24:47–48), though the transition from the Gospel to Acts is not without some awkwardness.[1] With Jesus' ascension and with the selection of a replacement for Judas, the stage is set for the next act.

Pentecost

THE NARRATIVE

The event that marks the transition from the time of Jesus to the time of the church is the coming of the Holy Spirit upon a small group in an upper room on the day of Pentecost. After such build-up, the event itself is recounted with remarkable brevity. The imagery is elusive. The disciples hear a sound "like" the rush of a mighty wind; there appear tongues "as of" fire. The distribution of fiery tongues and the coming of the wind (Greek: Spirit) clearly fulfill John's prophecy and Jesus' promise, but the narrative includes little interpretive detail.

Luke's description of the subsequent gathering of the crowd is equally vague. The testimony of the Spirit-filled apostles is described simply as "telling . . . the mighty works of God" (Acts 2:11). It is perhaps significant that the occasion is Pentecost. Luke may well assume that his readers know about the festival, known also as the Feast of Booths, one of the three pilgrimage festivals Jews were expected to celebrate in Jerusalem. It is obviously important that Jews from all over the world are present—and that they are all able to understand the testimony of the apostles in their own languages. Audience familiarity with traditions associated with Pentecost may account for the absence of interpretive detail.

Some scholars have pointed out that rabbinic sources, deriving from a later time, understand Pentecost not simply as a harvest festival but as a commemoration of the giving of the law on Mount Sinai.[2] If Pentecost and the giving of the law were associated at Luke's time, the declaration of God's mighty acts in every tongue would surely parallel legends about how the law, when given to Moses, was miraculously translated into every language under heaven.[3] Others have proposed that the narrator viewed the events as a counterpoint to the Tower of Babel in Genesis 11: the gift of God's Spirit reunites the scattered human family, enabling all to understand God's mighty acts manifest in Jesus.[4] Another possibility is to see in the story the fulfillment of prophecies about the restoration of the scattered people of Israel.

Some such traditional associations are likely. They would explain the interest in the list of countries from which the audience comes as well as the lack of interpretive detail. The author could assume knowledge on the part of his audience to which we do not have ready access. Precisely what ideas were associated with Pentecost must remain speculative, owing to the nature and date of sources. It is at least noteworthy that in the interpretation of Pentecost the author provides in Peter's speech, the variety of

languages has little significance. For Peter, and for Luke, the
meaning of Pentecost for the mission of Jesus' followers becomes
apparent only in light of other biblical passages and traditions.
Speaking in tongues is not an end in itself but a sign that a new era
has begun.

PETER'S SPEECH

Speeches are a prominent feature of Acts. Major addresses are
delivered by Peter, Stephen, and Paul. Scholars have focused
considerable attention on these speeches. Some have examined
them in light of speech writing among ancient historiographers.
Pioneering work was done by Martin Dibelius and Henry Cadbury.[5]
They argued convincingly that writing of history was not an exercise
for chroniclers but for those with a point of view. Speeches, they
pointed out, offered historians an opportunity both to display their
compositional skills and to impose their viewpoint on the story.
Speech writing was an essential ingredient in interpretation.
Though diversity among ancient historiographers makes general-
ization difficult, the high regard for speech writing among teachers
of historiography, the examples of Luke's contemporaries like
Josephus, and the prominence of speeches in Acts suggest that we
pay particular attention to the role of these major addresses in the
unfolding story of the early church.

Peter's first address begins as a response to misunderstanding.
Some in the crowd perceive only madness. They attribute the
strange behavior of the apostles to intoxication:

> But others mocking said, "They are filled with new wine." (Acts
> 2:13)

Peter offers a counter-interpretation: the event, he insists, must be
understood in light of biblical prophecy. The remarkable behavior
of the tongues-speakers fulfills a prophecy from Joel, which Peter
quotes:

> "And in the last days it shall be, God declares,
> that I will pour out my Spirit upon all flesh,
> and your sons and your daughters shall prophesy,
> and your young men shall see visions,

and your old men shall dream dreams;
yea, and on my menservants and my maidservants in those days
I will pour out my Spirit; and they shall prophesy.
And I will show wonders in the heavens above
and signs on the earth beneath,
blood, and fire, and vapor of smoke;
the sun shall be turned into darkness and the moon into blood
before the day of the Lord comes,
the great and manifest day.
And it shall be that whoever calls on the name of the Lord shall be
    saved." (Acts 2:17–21)

Several features of the quotation are notable. Most important is its interpretation of the inspired speech: it is characterized as prophecy. The Spirit poured out on Jesus' followers should be seen as the Spirit which inspired the prophets. According to Joel, in the "last days" God promised to pour out that Spirit not only on a select few but on "all flesh." By the first century, Jews believed that prophecy had ceased with Malachi and would resume only in the last times. Those times have arrived, Peter argues. The remarkable speech is evidence that God has poured out his Spirit. A new era of prophecy has begun: the "last days" have dawned.

A second notable feature of the quotation is that it ends prior to the obvious conclusion of the oracle in Joel. The citation, in fact, ceases in mid-sentence. The oracle in Joel continues:

"for in Mount Zion and in Jerusalem there shall be those who escape, as the Lord has said, and among the survivors shall be those whom the Lord calls." (Joel 2:32)

The abrupt ending of the citation prior to the natural end of the oracle must have some purpose. Why end with, "and it shall be that whoever calls on the name of the Lord shall be saved"?

A related question is posed by Acts 2:22. Peter addresses his audience again ("Men of Israel, hear these words. . . ."). On the one hand, the repeated address marks the end of the biblical quotation, necessary because the original Greek employed no punctuation marks. On the other hand, Peter seems to make an abrupt shift, speaking now about Jesus instead of the Spirit. Some commentators have argued that verse 22 marks a real break in the speech. It is more likely, however, that the strange ending of the quotation from Joel and the apparent shift in subject matter are related.

The passage from Joel speaks of the dawning of a new era, signaled by the outpouring of God's Spirit, when all will have an opportunity to "call on the name of the Lord" and be saved. The time of salvation has now arrived, Peter argues; that is the meaning of the tongues. Salvation will now be offered "in the name of the Lord." But who is the "Lord" in the text? In the Hebrew Bible there can be no question: the word translated "Lord" (RSV: LORD) is God's proper name, Jahweh. The Greek translations most Christians read, however, seem to have used the common Greek term for "lord" to translate God's name.[6] The discussion about Jesus that follows may suggest that the speaker reads "lord" in Joel as a reference to Jesus and understands the text to speak of salvation in Jesus' name. In fact, that is precisely what the speech seeks to prove.

The speech is an intricate argument, based on careful interpretation of biblical texts. Old Testament quotations and their interpretation provide the structure of the speech. The comments about Jesus in verses 22–24 make connections with the Joel citation. The "wonders" and "signs" God promises in Joel (Acts 2:19) point to the "signs and wonders" performed in Jesus' ministry (2:22). The promise that "the sun shall be turned into darkness" is fulfilled at Jesus' death (Luke 23:44). Comments about Jesus are followed by an extended quotation from Psalm 16. Like his contemporaries in the first century, the speaker assumes that psalms can be read as oracles, predicting the future. The quotation from the psalm, assumed to be from David, cannot be about David. The psalm refers to God's "Holy One" who will not see corruption; David died, however, and thus cannot be the "Holy One" referred to. The speaker assumes, again in light of other biblical evidence,[7] "Holy One" must be a designation for the Davidic Messiah, the descendant God promised to place on David's throne (Acts 2:30, with reference to Pss. 89 and 132). By raising Jesus from the dead, God fulfills the promise from the psalm—and identifies Jesus as the Messiah (Greek: Christ).

Peter's speech then takes another strange turn: "Being therefore exalted at the right hand of God." The concluding half-verse in Psalm 16, not quoted in Acts for some unknown reason, seems to explain the transition. "At thy right hand there are pleasures forever more," it reads (Ps. 16:11). Taken literally, the psalm locates the "Holy One" at God's right hand. It must therefore be about the exalted Holy One, or Christ, that Psalm 110:1 speaks, which explains Peter's quotation of the verse:

> "The Lord said to my Lord, Sit at my right hand,
> till I make thy enemies a stool for thy feet." (Acts 2:34–35)

In this verse the second figure is addressed as "Lord" by the Lord God. With the introduction of this verse, the speaker has proved his case:

> "Let all the house of Israel therefore know assuredly that God has
> made him both *Lord* and *Christ,* this Jesus whom you crucified."
> (Acts 2:36, emphasis added)

Having proved that Jesus can be called "Lord," Peter then proceeds to offer salvation to the crowd through baptism "in the name of Jesus Christ" (vs. 38). Jesus is the Lord in whose name salvation is offered, as prophesied by Joel. The speech now returns to the quotation from Joel, completing the oracle, in the reference to "every one whom the Lord our God calls to him" in Acts 2:39. The speech has come full circle.

Peter's speech, the first in Acts, provides the framework within which to understand the narrative as it unfolds. Current events are understood as the fulfillment of Joel's vision of the "last days." The era of prophecy has begun; long-awaited, the time of repentance and forgiveness is at hand. Those selected by Jesus to bear testimony gather the faithful remnant in Jerusalem, also foretold by Joel. The signs and wonders they perform offer evidence that the "last days" have indeed arrived and that the Spirit, poured out by the risen Jesus from his place at God's right hand, is at work. Other speeches fill in gaps and provide further detail, but the basic framework for Acts is complete. The speech is essential to the narrative; using Scripture and traditional language, it tells us what the story is about: the last days have arrived. The restoration of God's people has begun.

Two additional comments are in order. The first has to do with the value of the speech (and of the other speeches in Acts) as historical source material from which to recreate a picture of the actual career of the apostles. The speech is so intimately bound up with the program of Acts, so crucial to understanding the narrative as a whole, that it is difficult not to view the speech as a composition by the author of Acts. The intricate employment of scriptural texts reflects learned study of the Old Testament. Perhaps the most decisive evidence that the speech has been fashioned by Luke is that the proofs in the text and the connections between them depend upon the Greek Old Testament and not the Hebrew. Whatever historical kernel may lie at the heart of the narrative, in its present form the great speech at Pentecost most probably owes its existence to the artist who composed Acts. Many students of Acts believe the same to be true of other speeches in the book.

The second comment relates to the outlook. The speech is presented from a thoroughly Jewish perspective. Peter addresses an audience composed of Jews from all over the world, and his speech interprets the Jewish Bible. From the perspective of the Pentecost discourse at least, Jesus' coming, death, and resurrection have not led to the birth of a new religion. The outpouring of the Spirit signals a new era in the history of Israel, an era foreseen by the prophets. This is a time of restoration (Acts 1:6–8). What this has to do with Gentiles will become clear only later.

Emissaries of the Christ

The movement that began with Pentecost spread like wildfire across the face of the Roman Empire. The present title of Luke's second volume, "The Acts of the Apostles," was not original to the work and is somewhat misleading. The author seems less interested in sketching vivid portraits of past heores than in tracing the spectacular development of "the way." The story of its spread is largely the story of a handful of characters. The list includes Peter, James, John, Philip, Stephen, and Paul. Philip and James play important roles in the drama but are devoid of personality; John is

Peter's silent companion, never emerging from the shadows. Stephen takes the stage long enough to deliver a major address, then disappears. Only Peter and Paul could be termed credible characters. Yet even in the case of the two major figures, speeches are highly stereotyped. There is little to distinguish Peter's missionary speeches from Paul's. The only singular addresses are Paul's speech on the Areopagus (Acts 17) and those offered in his own defense (chapters 22—26). Individuality emerges only in the narratives, and even here there is considerable stereotyping.

Though Luke invests little in character development, he is still interested in the role of emissary or apostle. The role or office seems at least as important to him as those who fill it. The function of these emissaries or apostles has been carefully detailed in his Gospel.
Luke 6:12–16. Jesus selects from a larger group of disciples twelve he calls "apostles" (or emissaries). Little is said about their mission except that they will be sent out.
Luke 9:1–5. Jesus sends the twelve on a preaching mission, giving them "power and authority over all demons and to cure diseases." He sends them "to preach the kingdom of God and to heal." Their commission seems identical to his (see 4:18–19).
Luke 10:1–16. Jesus sends out seventy (or seventy-two) to prepare for his coming as he journeys to Jerusalem. The emissaries receive elaborate instructions about the conduct of their mission. "He who hears you hears me," says Jesus, "and he who rejects you rejects me, and he who rejects me rejects him who sent me." The apostle speaks with the authority of the one who sends him.
Luke 12:8–12. Defining "blasphemy against the Holy Spirit," Jesus distinguishes between speaking against the Son of man (himself), a sin that can be forgiven, and blasphemy against the Holy Spirit, which cannot be forgiven. The meaning of the latter is explained in the verses that follow immediately:

> "And when they bring you before the synagogues and the rulers and the authorities, do not be anxious how or what you are to answer or what you are to say; for the Holy Spirit will teach you in that very hour what you ought to say."

Refusal to accept the testimony of the Spirit-filled apostles offered after the time of "ignorance" has ended (Acts 3:17–19 and 17:30–31), constitutes "blasphemy against the Holy Spirit."

Luke 21:12–19. In the course of an address about the future, Jesus tells his followers what they can expect from people in authority: they will be imprisoned and forced to appear before synagogues, kings, and governors. Jesus promises that he will empower their testimony, giving them "a mouth and wisdom, which none of your adversaries will be able to withstand or contradict." And in a statement of immense significance for the story Acts tells, Jesus makes his followers a solemn promise: "But not a hair of your head will perish" (vs. 18). Stories of miraculous escapes punctuate Acts, demonstrating the fulfillment of his promise.

Luke 22:28–30. In a discourse at the Last Supper, Jesus makes extravagant promises to his disciples:

> You are those who have continued with me in my trials; as my Father appointed a kingdom for me [or kingly authority], so do I appoint for you that you may eat and drink at my table in my kingdom, and sit on thrones judging the twelve tribes of Israel.

A twelfth apostle is necessary after Judas' demise so that there will be a ruler for each of Israel's twelve tribes (Acts 1:12–26).

Luke 24:46–49. In a passage discussed earlier, the role of the apostles is set forth in the context of what has "been written." They are to preach repentance and forgiveness to all nations, beginning in Jerusalem. The promise of power from on high provides a direct link to the story of Pentecost.

PETER

More than anyone else, Peter embodies the ideal of an apostle so carefully prepared in the Gospel. There is little reason to expect much of Peter, an untrained speaker and a fisherman by trade. Whatever promise he may have shown was destroyed by his performance at Jesus' trial (Luke 22:54–62). Yet Peter, like his fellow disciples, was forgiven and restored to fellowship with Jesus. And with the coming of the Spirit at Pentecost, Peter is transformed into a true leader. His first speech is an immense success, resulting in the conversion of three thousand people. The common fisherman soon attracts the attention of the leaders—as Jesus promised. He and John are interrogated, beaten, and finally imprisoned—but to no avail. Even jails cannot hold them (Acts 5:17–26). So popular is Peter that the chief priests cannot mistreat him for fear of being stoned (Acts 5:26).

Stories of Peter's successes are remarkably unrestrained. Like Jesus, he heals cripples and even raises the dead. Some of the comments made about Peter surpass anything said about Jesus:

> And more than ever believers were added to the Lord, multitudes both of men and women, so that they even carried out the sick into the streets, and laid them on beds and pallets, that as Peter came by at least his shadow might fall on some of them. (Acts 5:14–15)

The point of the story, however, is not the inherent greatness of Peter or his comrades. His eloquence testifies to the presence of the Spirit:

> Now when they saw the boldness of Peter and John, and perceived that they were uneducated, common men, they wondered; and they recognized that they had been with Jesus. (Acts 4:13)

It is the Spirit, poured out on the apostles by Jesus himself, that explains the remarkable transformation and the immense success of the new movement. Again and again we are told that Peter and John depend not on their own resources: they heal "in the name of Jesus of Nazareth" (Acts 3:6; cf. 4:10). They speak boldly because the Spirit "gives them utterance" (Acts 2:4). They are delivered from their enemies in fulfillment of Jesus' promise. Ironically, it is a respected leader of the Jews, Gamaliel, who in his speech to the Sanhedrin, provides for us an interpretation of what is occurring.

> "Men of Israel, take care what you do with these men. For before these days Theudas arose, giving himself out to be somebody, and a number of men, about four hundred, joined him; but he was slain and all who followed him were dispersed and came to nothing. After him Judas the Galilean arose. . . . So in the present case I tell you, keep away from these men and let them alone; for if this plan or this undertaking is of men, it will fail; but if it is of God, you will not be able to overthrow them. You might even be found opposing God!" (Acts 5:35–39)

The theme of the opening chapters may perhaps be termed the triumph of the Spirit—the Spirit who speaks and acts through Peter and the rest of the apostles. A new era has begun, heralded by those who witness to Jesus' resurrection. The momentum created in Jerusalem will carry the mission to the ends of the earth, against all odds. Those who unsuccessfully seek to oppose the apostles are indeed opposing God. In refusing the testimony of those through whom the Spirit of God speaks, the leaders of the people forfeit their right to be leaders and commit blasphemy against the Spirit and God. The twelve replace them as Israel's true leaders.

Peter dominates the first half of Acts as the typical bearer of the Spirit, performing signs and wonders, delivering critical addresses. He also plays a crucial role as the "liberal" within the Jerusalem church. Ironically, Peter—who, Paul says, was entrusted with the "gospel to the circumcised" (Gal. 2:7)—appears in Acts as the first missionary to the uncircumcised. Even in Acts it is not obvious that this should have been the case. In chapters 6—7, the author cryptically describes a controversy between "Hellenists" and "Hebrews" that results in the appointment of seven deacons. After one of them, Stephen, is martyred, the rest are driven out of Jerusalem. (The text says the persecution is against "the church," but since Peter and the rest are still in Jerusalem later, apparently the persecution is directed against a particular segment of the movement, the Hellenists. See Acts 8:1.) One of those driven out, Philip, preaches to the Samaritans—not yet Gentiles, but clearly an exception to the preaching thus far. We learn that some of the scattered Hellenists found their way to Antioch, where they "spoke to the Greeks also" (Acts 11:19–20). The story of the dispersed preachers, however, breaks off with Philip and is picked up only later (Acts 11:19ff.). Their story is interrupted by the conversion of Paul, the renowned missionary to the Gentiles. However, before continuing Paul's story, the author breaks off again, this time to tell how Peter came to convert Cornelius (chapter 10). Whether or not this Gentile is chronologically the first to be converted, in Acts his conversion marks the formal beginning of a new direction. And Peter is the prime mover.

Peter is not naturally disposed to visit Cornelius. We know from
Cornelius' vision (Acts 10:3–6) that God intends Peter to come. Only
after three visions in which God cleanses what is unclean, and a direct
communication from the Spirit (Acts 10:19–20), does Peter agree to
go along. Peter reluctantly enters the Gentile's house, but expresses
his reservations as a good Jew (Acts 10:28–29). He preaches a brief
sermon in which he stresses what God has done "for the people
[Jews]" that is interrupted by an outpouring of the Holy Spirit.

> And the believers from among the circumcised who came with Peter
> were amazed, because the gift of the Holy Spirit had been poured
> out even on the Gentiles. (Acts 10:45)

Peter is literally forced to baptize Cornelius and his household and
to welcome them into the family of God—as Gentiles.

Upon his return to Jerusalem Peter is attacked by "the
circumcision party" for having eaten with the uncircumcised (Acts
11:2–3). The issue is not whether Gentiles are to be permitted to
share in the gospel but on what conditions. The Torah forbids social
intercourse, yet Peter has eaten with Gentiles. Peter's story about
his vision and about God's pouring out the Spirit on Gentiles, thus
cleansing them, settles the matter for the moment.

The issue comes up once more, this time more formally, in
chapter 15, at the so-called "Apostolic Council." The occasion now
seems to be the ministry of the church in Antioch, specifically the
ministries of Paul and Barnabas. This is presumably the same
conference Paul describes in Galatians 2. In Acts, however, the
primary figure at the conference is Peter, whose recounting of his
visit to Cornelius offers James the opportunity to make a decision
about Gentiles, supporting his view with scriptural quotations. As
Luke tells the story, Paul has virtually no role to play in the
conference or in the decision.

We shall return to the Jew/Gentile question in a later chapter.
We note here only the central role Peter plays in the mission to
non-Jews. In Acts, the "liberal" decisions about the inclusion of
Gentiles are made by Peter and James, characters whose Jewish
credentials are beyond reproach.[8] Peter is important thus not simply
as the typical bearer of the Spirit and leader of the apostolic circle,

but as a reliable Jew whose prestige serves to legitimize the inclusion of Gentiles in "the way" without circumcision. The rather different picture of the conference and of Peter's role Paul provides in his letter to the Galatians only heightens the significance of Peter's role for understanding the perspective of Acts.

STEPHEN

In the first five chapters Peter is the main character, healing the sick, converting thousands by his preaching, and presiding over the growing number within the new sect in Jerusalem. Despite the irritation of Sadducees, who do not believe in the resurrection and thus resent the preaching of the apostles (Acts 4:2), the movement flourishes. Troubles are from the outside and do little to stem the tide of conversions.

Chapter 6 marks a transition. The new movement experiences growing pains: "the Hellenists murmured against the Hebrews" (Acts 6:1). The author provides no information about the identity of the two groups. The terms probably refer to Greek-speaking and Aramaic-speaking Jews. The Greek names of the seven "deacons" selected from the Hellenists, and the information that one is a proselyte from Antioch (Acts 6:5), support such a reading. The nature of the dispute is unclear. The problem is ostensibly that some feel that goods are being distributed unequally. The deacons, however, are obviously more than financial managers chosen to "serve tables." Stephen and Philip are actively engaged in evangelism. The problems were clearly more complex than Luke reveals, perhaps reflecting deep divisions within Jerusalem society between various parties. Such divisions were almost certainly reflected in the Christian movement, for when the great persecution arises against the church as a result of Stephen's execution, the only ones driven out appear to be the Hellenists. The nature of the dispute will continue to elicit a variety of interpretations from scholars until more is known about first-century Jewish society.

Stephen, the second major character in Acts, is abruptly introduced as one of the deacons; we learn only that he is "full of grace and power" and that he "did great wonders and signs among the people." Though not one of the twelve, he is actively engaged in a mission to diaspora Jews in the city of Jerusalem (Acts 6:9). His preaching stirs up controversy that is eventually brought to the high court. The issue is not the resurrection, as with Peter and John. Stephen is accused of apostasy and blasphemy, the first time such a charge is leveled at believers in Jesus:

> Then they secretly instigated men, who said, "We have heard him speak blasphemous words against Moses and God." (Acts 6:11)

Stephen is brought to trial on charges of heresy:

> "This man never ceases to speak words against this holy place and the law; for we have heard him say that this Jesus of Nazareth will destroy this place, and will change the customs which Moses delivered to us." (Acts 6:13–14)

The charges, remarkably similar to those offered by "false witnesses" at Jesus' trial as described in Matthew and Mark, provide the occasion for Stephen's speech, the longest in Acts. The speech serves as his defense.

The lengthy oration comes at a critical juncture in the story. It marks the transition from a mission to inhabitants in Jerusalem to a mission to Samaritans and to Jews of the diaspora, eventually to Gentiles. More is at stake than the fate of Stephen. He is important less as a missionary than as an interpreter of the tradition and of the imminent crisis within the Jewish community. What does it mean that leaders of the people of Israel condemn Stephen as an apostate? One of the charges against Stephen is that he speaks against the temple. According to Luke, Jesus predicted that the temple would be destroyed (Luke 21:5–24). Is it possible that Jesus and his followers were apostates, heretics who rejected their heritage and had forfeited the right to be called children of Abraham? What opposition to the temple is apparent, and does such opposition imply an attack on the whole Jewish way of life? The speech intends to answer such questions in a programmatic way. As with Peter's opening speech at Pentecost, Stephen's address seeks to provide a framework within which to understand the events of the present—and the future.[9]

Stephen's oration is different from any that precede it in Acts. It is not a missionary speech, intended to win converts. Nor is it a careful exposition of biblical passages. It is a recital of the past, a historical survey of a type familiar from the Old Testament, reminiscent of Joshua's address to the gathered tribes (Josh. 24) or of Ezra's prayer in Nehemiah 9 or of Daniel's prayer in Daniel 9, perhaps even of the recital in Psalm 78. As with other surveys, certain events are selected as illustrative of the main point of the address; the dynamics of the story are linked to the purpose of the speech—the recital intends to make some specific impact on the audience, perhaps calling for a particular response. Comparison with other recitals may clarify the distinctiveness of the review in Acts 7 and may shed light on its function.

Joshua's speech, the simplest of the recitals, makes one point: everything the tribes possess has been given by God. He cleared the land, delivered them from bondage, and gave them a place. All he requests in return is single-minded allegiance. The recital of God's mighty acts on behalf of the people leads directly to the choice Joshua lays before the people: put away foreign gods and serve the God who has fought for you (Josh. 24:15).

Psalm 78, like revisionist history after the American Civil War, tells the story of God's people from a southern perspective, using the destruction of the Northern Kingdom by the Assyrians (721 B.C.E.) as a lesson in the wages of disobedience. God's purpose for the people, according to the speaker, led directly to the selection of David as king and to the establishment of his dynasty. The recital conveys a rather different picture of what it means to be one of God's chosen, urging fidelity to the Davidic family and to the religious institution in Jerusalem.

Ezra's and Daniel's prayers both look back on the history of God's people as a story of disobedience. The recital is a litany of rebellions which have brought devastation to Israel. Ezra, however, focuses on the giving of the law as the focal point of Israel's history, virtually ignoring the era of the kings, closing with a sweeping call for ritual purity. Daniel sees the city of Jerusalem as the clearest embodiment of God's promises to Israel and closes with an impassioned prayer for its restoration to former glory.

The recitals are distinctive, reflecting differing conceptions of identity and a variety of hopes for the future. The beginning of the survey, the ending, the selection of events all serve to elicit from the audience some particular response. The same is true of the speech in Acts 7.

The story Stephen tells begins with Abraham, "our father," and with a promise from God: "Depart . . . and go into the land which I will show you." The promise that sets the story in motion, however, is made in verse 7. Abraham is told that his posterity will be blessed only after a period of bondage:

> "But I will judge the nation which they serve," said God, "and after that they shall come out and worship me in this place." (Acts 7:7)

The subsequent history of Abraham's family is the unfolding of this promise. The question is what God meant by "this place." One answer might be Mount Sinai, so that the giving of the law at Sinai would constitute the fulfillment of God's promise. An even more widespread interpretation within Jewish tradition would see the building of the temple as the fulfillment; "the place" in Deuteronomy is virtually synonymous with the temple on Mount Zion, the "place" God chose to dwell forever (see Ps. 132:14). As we shall see, Stephen locates the fulfillment of the promise elsewhere.

The selection of events from Israel's history is unusual. Stephen recounts nothing from the sagas of Isaac and Jacob, but does tell about Joseph, an interesting but hardly central figure from Israel's past. The story is important for two reasons. First, it tells how God's promises about enslavement and ill treatment were fulfilled; secondly, it introduces a theme that runs throughout the story: conflict within the family. The patriarchs, jealous of Joseph, sold him into slavery. Even then the family of Abraham was divided against itself. Fortunately for posterity, God was with Joseph, and the worst efforts of his brothers only served to further God's plans. The theme of rejection and vindication will recur in the story.

Most of the narrative is devoted to Moses and again, two different themes appear. Moses is chosen to lead the children of Abraham out of bondage. "As the time of the promise drew near,"

God raised up Moses. The narrator pauses, however, to tell of Moses' first rejection by his own people (Acts 7:23–29): "Who made you a ruler and a judge over us?" his brethren say to him. The answer is provided: God made him ruler and deliverer (Acts 7:35). The initial rejection of Moses foreshadows what is to occur later in the wilderness. Even while Moses is on Mount Sinai receiving the law, his people are building an idol:

> Our fathers refused to obey him, but thrust him aside, and in their hearts they returned to Egypt. . . . (Acts 7:39)

Rather than obeying Moses, whom God had appointed ruler and deliverer, "our fathers" offered a sacrifice to the idol and "rejoiced in the works of their hands" (Acts 7:41).

Moses is both the agent of fulfilling God's promises in the past and the type of the deliverer to come:

> This is the Moses who said to the Israelites, "God will raise up for you a prophet from your brethren as he raised me up." (Acts 7:37)

In Peter's speech in Acts 3, Jesus is explicitly identified as the prophet like Moses (Acts 3:22–23). Like Moses, Jesus performed signs and wonders (Acts 2:22 and 7:36); like Moses, he was rejected by some of his brethren. The pattern of opposition rising from the story of Israel applies to the present as well:

> "You stiff-necked people, uncircumcised in heart and ears, you always resist the Holy Spirit. As *your* fathers did, so do you. Which of the prophets did not *your* fathers persecute? And they killed those who announced beforehand the coming of the Righteous One, whom you have now betrayed and murdered, you who received the law as delivered by angels and did not keep it." (Acts 7:51–53, emphasis added)

Jesus and his emissaries stand in a long tradition of rejected spokespersons of God. The family of Israel, according to this survey, has always been split, with one segment consistently rejecting those selected by God to lead and to speak for God—leaders and spokespersons vindicated by God. In rejecting Jesus and his emissaries like Stephen, leaders of the Jews oppose the Holy Spirit (see above) and show themselves to be descended from

the branch of the family that has always rejected God. They, not
Stephen and those for whom he speaks, are false Jews, betrayers of
the tradition; they, not Stephen, are guilty of blaspheming God's
Spirit.

The speech focuses on another aspect of the story of Israel
directly related to the situation of Stephen: the temple. As noted
above, some interpreters saw God's appearance to Moses at Sinai as
the fulfillment of his promise of worship "in this place." That is not
said in Stephen's speech, however. Rather, Stephen describes the
"tent of witness" as the place of worship during the wilderness
wanderings. The tent was the "place" of worship until David
brought it to Jerusalem and Solomon built the temple. In Rabbinic
thought, and according to Davidic theology in Kings, Deuteronomy, and in royal psalms, the building of the temple is the
fulfillment of God's promise to Abraham. Mount Zion is the place
God has chosen to dwell; this is now the place where God is to be
worshiped. According to Stephen, however, that is a serious
misunderstanding. God does not dwell in houses:

> "Yet the Most High does not dwell in houses made with hands; as
> the prophet says,
>> 'Heaven is my throne,
>> and earth my footstool.
>> What house will you build for me, says the Lord,
>> or what is the place of my rest?
>> Did not my hand make all these things?' " (Acts 7:49–50)

Stephen, like the rabbis, notes the contrast in Isaiah's words
between what is built by God's hands and by the hands of humans.
Unlike the rabbis, he chooses to go no further than Isaiah: God does
not dwell in houses. It cannot be, therefore, that the building of
Solomon's temple represents the fulfillment of God's promise of a
"place" of worship. The conclusion of the historical survey with
Solomon's building of the temple and the quotation from Isaiah
focuses on the disputed matter: is the temple an essential
component in Jewish identity? Does predicting the destruction of
the temple constitute apostasy?

Stephen's answer—and Luke's—is obviously no. Scripture itself prevents such an interpretation. In fact, in preferring a building "made with hands" to the prophet like Moses and his emissaries, leaders of the people make of the temple an idol. Like their fathers who worshiped the work of their hands (Acts 7:41), they will be punished. The quotation from Amos issues a thinly-veiled threat:

> "But God turned and gave them over to worship the host of heaven, as it is written in the book of the prophets:
>   'Did you offer to me slain beasts and sacrifices,
>   forty years in the wilderness, O house of Israel?
> And you took up the tent of Moloch,
> and the star of the god Rephan,
> the figures which you made to worship;
> and I will remove you beyond Babylon.'" (Acts 7:42–43)

The temple, a building made with hands, is apparently like the "tent" of Moloch—a contrast to the real "tent of witness," the proper place of worship. Though the interpretation is not carried through consistently, the reference to the "fallen tent of David" God has raised up (Acts 15:16) provides the true interpretation of the initial promise to Abraham. The true "place" of worship is wherever two or three are gathered in Jesus's name; it is in the homes of those who repent and believe in Jesus, who accept salvation in his name, that God is properly worshiped. It is among those repentant Jews who believe the words of the prophet like Moses and his emissaries that God's promises continue to be fulfilled, promises that will eventually encompass Jews from all over the world and even Gentiles (see Acts 15:16–17).

Using the medium of historical survey, the speech communicates a sense of identity to those who, like Stephen, find themselves at odds with brothers and sisters within the Jewish family. Such opposition is nothing new; in fact, in light of the story Stephen tells, opposition may even be confirmation that Jews who are persecuted for believing in Jesus stand in the tradition of Moses and the prophets. The speech also provides a sketch of Jewish identity which makes the temple unnecessary. There is no sustained polemic against sacrifice as such, no thorough indictment of the present leadership. The apostles worship in the temple. The point seems to be that the temple is not the end of the story, that it was never intended to be God's "resting place forever." In their refusal to accept Jesus and his emissaries, in their blind devotion to the temple and defense of it against Stephen and Paul (see chapter 21), its leaders forfeit their right to serve as leaders; they deny their own heritage, even blaspheme the Spirit. They, not Stephen, are guilty of faithlessness to the tradition. Readers of Acts could understand the destruction of the temple by the Romans in 70 C.E. as confirmation of God's rejection of the temple and its leaders. The framework for understanding that destruction and for understanding Jewish identity without a temple is provided preeminently in Stephen's address.

Luke thus offered for his readers an interpretation of the past as did teachers within the Jewish community. Rabbinic Judaism and Christianity, said one scholar, were two Jewish sects able to survive the destruction of the temple. Interpretations differ at a crucial point, however. For the rabbis, the temple was destroyed because of *our* sins and the sins of *our* fathers; for Luke, it is because of *your* sins and the sins of *your* fathers. There has been a decisive parting of the way which this speech, and all of Acts, seeks to interpret.

Stephen's defense is unsuccessful; in fact, it insures his execution, making him the first martyr. The execution, and the resulting expulsion of the Hellenists, does nothing to disrupt the movement, however. On the contrary, "those who were scattered went about preaching the word" (Acts 8:4). Philip evangelizes Samaritans, others find their way to Antioch where they preach the gospel even to Gentiles (Acts 11:19–26). The church at Antioch becomes a major force in organizing Paul's mission. Ironically, the efforts by the Jewish leaders serve only to spread the gospel. It is as Joseph told his brothers: "As for you, you meant evil against me; but God meant it for good" (Gen. 50:20). And it is as Gamaliel said: ". . . if this plan or this undertaking is of men, it will fail; but if it is of God, you will not be able to overthrow them. You might even be found opposing God!" (Acts 5:38–39).

As with Peter's speeches, Stephen's address is so crucial to the program of Acts, its outlook so completely in accord with that of Luke-Acts as a whole, that it is difficult not to see the speech as a composition of the author.

PAUL

Of all the characters in Acts, Paul is the most interesting. His career occupies half the narrative. Though one of the central emissaries of Christ, Paul is an exception to most rules. He was not among Jesus' followers. In fact, he begins his career as a notorious persecutor of Christians, implicated in the execution of Stephen. Unlike Peter, whose troubles stem from a few hostile religious leaders, Paul stirs up controversy everywhere in almost every circle. He is in and out of prison; once he is stoned and left for dead. Jews are enraged at his preaching, some dogging his steps across the empire as far as Jerusalem. Paul has major disagreements even with Barnabas, his companion. His life is endangered during his first visit to Jerusalem. His second visit apparently settles a major controversy which is rekindled during his third visit, resulting in his arrest. Even Jewish Christians in Jerusalem are troubled by what they hear of Paul's teachings.

Stranger yet is Paul's trial, an affair that drags on for six chapters. During its course several Roman leaders indicate that Paul has committed no crime against Roman law. The extended speeches Paul offers in his defense focus not on political charges but on questions of his "orthodoxy," matters the Romans find incomprehensible. The story ends without reporting the conclusion of the trial, though the author and his audience certainly know that Paul was executed. While Luke could not tell the story of the church without devoting a lengthy chapter to its greatest missionary, Paul requires special treatment. Some have even termed the second half of Acts an apology for Paul.

Historical difficulties. We are in the remarkably fortunate position of possessing not only a full record of Paul's career in Acts but several letters penned by the great apostle himself. Some comparing of biography and letters is thus inevitable. Remarkably little comparison is done, however, in popular works on Paul. Maps of Paul's travels in the back of Bibles come directly from Acts. Paul never gives the impression in his letters that his travels were divided into district "journeys," though that is the way they are arranged in Acts.[10] Stories of Paul's conversion are typically lifted directly from Acts 9, with virtually no attention to Philippians 3 or Galatians 1. One reason is perhaps the conviction, of long standing, that Acts was written by one who traveled with Paul (note especially the "we" passages beginning in Acts 16).

There are some historical difficulties. One has to do with Paul's relations with the Jerusalem church. According to Paul's account of his travels in Galatians 1, he went to Jerusalem for the first time three years after his conversion. On that occasion he saw only Peter and James, the Lord's brother (Gal. 1:15–19). The next fourteen years he spent, he says, in Syria and Cilicia (Gal. 1:21–22). His second trip to Jerusalem was for the purpose of settling questions about the legitimacy of his mission to Gentiles and the unity of the church—a meeting, Paul insists, that ended with a formal acknowledgement of his ministry by the "pillars" (Gal. 2:9–10).

Acts offers a rather different picture. Paul's base of operation is Jerusalem, where he is not only known but is an official delegate of the council with authority to arrest believers in Jesus. Soon after his conversion, he returns to Jerusalem where he is introduced to the apostles by Barnabas (Acts 9:27). During the course of his first visit he preaches, stirring up trouble with "Hellenists"—perhaps the same Greek-speaking Jews Stephen antagonized. In danger of his life, Paul flees.

His second visit, for the so-called "Apostolic Conference," is occasioned by a dispute within the church at Antioch. Paul is simply one of the delegates. The decision reached by the council has virtually nothing to do with Paul's testimony; it is based rather on Peter's experience with Cornelius and on James' reading of Scripture. The Gentile policy involves Paul's mission, but it is by no means a ratification of Paul's approach. Indeed, the council issues a decree imposing on Gentiles observance of certain features of the Torah (eating kosher meat and abstaining from gross immorality) that will enable table fellowship with Jewish Christians without violating the Torah—an agreement to which Paul never refers in his letters.[11]

The passages are symptomatic of other important differences. Paul introduces himself as the Apostle to the Gentiles in Romans 1:5; in Galatians 2:7, he speaks of himself as having been "entrusted with the gospel to the uncircumcised, just as Peter had been entrusted with the gospel to the circumcised." In Acts, Paul is called to preach both to Jews and Gentiles (Acts 9:15). Paul's understanding of the Jewish law, its relationship to the gospel, and its bearing on his mission to non-Jews, so central to his message in Galatians and Romans, is largely absent from Acts.

A proper comparison of the Paul of Acts with the Paul of the letters would require a lengthy volume, many of which have already been written. Acts certainly contains much that is historically reliable; it also differs significantly from Paul on important matters, focusing primarily on those relating to Jewish tradition. It is sufficient in this study to call attention to the differences. Since the purpose of this chapter is to examine the role of Paul in Acts, we may leave unresolved questions about the "historical Paul."

Paul's journeys. If the story of Acts tells of the spread of the gospel to the end of the earth, Paul is the primary agent of that mission. His extraordinary career will take him across Asia Minor, through Greece, and eventually to Rome. It is in this sense that Paul is atypical of the major figures in Acts. He is always on the move, making whirlwind journeys by land and sea, constrained by the Spirit to avoid certain areas, invited in visions to visit others. Unlike Peter and Stephen and Philip, Paul operates regularly on the boundaries of the Jewish community. Though he begins at synagogues, Paul readily leaves to work with God-fearers. Acts may not portray Paul exclusively as a missionary to Gentiles, but he is the only major character to work so frequently with non-Jews. Even if the story provides few specifics, what God is doing among the Gentiles is largely what God is doing through Paul.

Given the amount of space devoted to Paul's travels, it is somewhat remarkable how few specifics the author provides. Stories of Paul's deeds do little to set him apart from Luke's ideal apostles, like Peter. Paul performs signs and wonders. He heals the sick, exorcises demons, even raises the dead. Some are so impressed they hail him as a god (Acts 14:8–18); so awesome are his powers that a whole town is moved to bring books on magic and to burn them publicly (Acts 19:17–20). Though imprisoned, stoned, shipwrecked, and bitten by a poisonous serpent, Paul survives—fulfilling Jesus' prediction that "not a hair of your head will perish" (Luke 21:18).

Like Peter and Stephen, Paul delivers speeches. Filled with the Holy Spirit, his eloquence is unmatched. Opponents cannot withstand his arguments. The great missionary even delivers an address on the famed Areopagus in Athens, the citadel of classical culture (Acts 17). People respond to Paul's preaching as to Peter's: some believe, some do not. Once again there is little in Paul's speeches to distinguish him from other of Christ's emissaries.

Even Paul's travels have been stereotyped to some extent. Often the narrator mentions the name of the city or town where he preaches, noting that Paul began his preaching in the synagogue (Acts 13:5, 14; 14:1; 17:1–2, 10–11, 17; 18:4, 19). Sometimes he gives the names of people with whom Paul stayed (Acts 16:14–15; 18:1–3). On some occasions the author includes anecdotes, on others speeches. Sometimes, however, no details are provided. In Acts 16:6–10, for example, Luke tells of Paul's travels through Asia Minor and eventually to Macedonia. Apart from the mention of the regions of Galatia and Phrygia and Mysia and Bithynia, there is scarcely a detail. We are not told how Paul was prevented by the Holy Spirit from speaking in Asia or from traveling north to Bithynia (Acts 16:6–7). The authors says not a word about Paul's ministry among the "churches of Galatia," to whom Paul wrote a letter. In that letter Paul refers to an ailment that forced him to stay in Galatia and that provided the occasion for his preaching there (Gal. 4:12–15). Perhaps in retrospect Paul could refer to his ailment as constraint by the Spirit.

It is possible that Luke provides few details in such narratives because his sources were deficient.[12] At least as important, however, is the impression the story makes in its present form: through Paul, the gospel is carried across the face of the empire. The mission moves through Asia Minor to Greece and, finally, to Rome. It is the Spirit that provides the motive force. Paul is merely the instrument by which Jesus' promise is fulfilled: "in all Judea and Samaria and to the end of the earth" (Acts 1:8). The same providence that governed the careers of Jesus and Peter and Stephen directs Paul's. This too has been "written" (Luke 24:46–47).

In one final sense, Paul serves as an embodiment of an ideal in Acts: he suffers.[13] In the account of his conversion is a thematic statement that anticipates his career. Ananias, a disciple in Damascus, is told in a vision to lay hands on Paul. In response to his objection, God tells him:

> "Go, for he is a chosen instrument of mine to carry my name before the Gentiles and kings and the sons of Israel; for I will show him how much he must suffer for the sake of my name." (Acts 9:15)

His career fulfills the prediction. Plots against Paul's life are formed in Damascus and in Jerusalem. In Lystra, Paul is stoned and left for dead (Acts 14:19). He is beaten and imprisoned in Philippi (Acts 16:19–24), forced to flee Thessalonica (Acts 17:5–10). Wherever he goes Paul stirs up trouble, leading eventually to his arrest in Jerusalem.

Like Stephen, Paul offers some interpretation of the opposition he will face at the beginning of his ministry. His first major speech in Antioch of Pisidia (Acts 13:16–41), a speech with the same programmatic significance as Stephen's address and Peter's Pentecost discourse, concludes with a scriptural comment on the reception he expects. The quotation from Habakkuk introduces a note of warning into Paul's diaspora mission:

> "Behold, you scoffers, and wonder, and perish;
> for I do a deed in your days,
> a deed you will never believe, if one declares it to you." (Acts 13:40)

Like his contemporaries at Qumran, on the shores of the Dead Sea, Paul assumes that the prophetic passage was addressed to his time.[14] He is the one appointed by God to "declare" the gospel. Some in the audience, however, will scoff and will never believe; they are the "you" foreseen by the prophet. The citation again provides a means of understanding opposition to Paul. Those who refuse the message he brings fulfill Scripture in their opposition—and they will perish. The pattern was established early in Acts: salvation awaits those

who believe in Jesus (Acts 2:21, quoting Joel); those who refuse to
heed the words of the prophet like Moses forefeit their right to be
called children of Abraham and will be "rooted out" (Acts 3:22–23,
quoting Deut. 18, author's translation). The establishment of a
remnant of "true Jews," joined by pious Gentiles, begun in
Jerusalem by Peter, continues in the ministry of Paul throughout the
diaspora.

Arrest and trial. For many, chapters 21—28 in Acts are an anomaly.
Prior to this, Jesus' emissaries fulfill their commission by carrying
the message of repentance and forgiveness in Jesus' name across the
empire. Congregations have been established in Judea, Samaria,
Syria, Cilicia, Asia Minor, and Greece. Yet suddenly the mission
comes to a halt—or at least the narrator breaks off the story. In Acts
19:21, Paul announces his plans to visit Jerusalem and from there to
head west to Rome. No explanations are given, though gaps can be
filled in from Paul's letters.[15] When trouble erupts in Ephesus, Paul
takes his leave—though he heads not for Jerusalem but Greece.
After several months, Paul crosses the Aegean and begins his
fateful trip to Jerusalem. The formal farewell speech delivered to
elders from the church at Ephesus (20:17–35) marks the end of
Paul's career as a missionary. He goes on to Jerusalem, as if under
some compulsion, knowing that trouble awaits him there (21:11–
14). The prophecies of trouble prove correct. Paul is arrested, and
the rest of the story recounts his trial and his eventual appeal to
Rome (chapters 22—28).

Reasons for the extended account of Paul's trial are unclear.
One difficulty is that the trial is never resolved. Acts ends with Paul
in Rome, awaiting the final disposition of his case. Unless Acts was
written before Paul's trial was completed, which is most unlikely,
the failure to resolve the trial may indicate an interest that is more
than biographical.

Some scholars have argued, for example, that the author is not
really interested in Paul's guilt or innocence. Paul, they argue,
embodies the new "Christian" movement. Roman officials must
now decide how to regard the new movement. Should believers in
Jesus be considered Jews, in which case they deserve the same legal
guarantees to worship accorded other Jews? Or are they to be

viewed as adherents of a new—and illegal—religious movement? According to this interpretation, Paul's trial offers the author of Acts an opportunity to argue the political case for the right of Christians to worship.

Several questions arise. Paul's trial seems a strange vehicle for such an appeal to Roman authorities, particularly since the outcome surely went against Paul. The story reports no legal vindication of Paul in Rome—nor could it. According to tradition, Paul was martyred in Rome. Further, an argument for the legal status of Christians under Roman law cannot be fit easily into the thematic development of Luke-Acts. Though it is not impossible that these chapters are an appendage, an interpretation that could link the trial account with an overall plan of Luke-Acts would seem preferable. Finally, there is little about legal matters in the lengthy trial narrative. Romans insist from the beginning that Paul has committed no crime (Acts 23:26–30; 25:14–22, 24–27). Festus admits that if Paul had not appealed to Rome he would have had to free him (26:30–32). Paul's lengthy speeches simply dismiss political matters and focus on his relationship to Jewish tradition, matters which Roman officials cannot understand (Acts 23:29; 25:18–20). Paul's speeches are ill-conceived as apologies directed to Roman officials.

A more plausible interpretation of Paul's trial, argued cogently by Jacob Jervell,[16] links the trial with opposition Paul has encountered from hostile Jews throughout his ministry. The opposition climaxes in chapter 21 with Paul's arrest. Even the elders of the Jerusalem church are uneasy about Paul's visit in light of rumors spread about his teaching:

> And they said to him, "You see, brother, how many thousands there are among the Jews of those who have believed; they are all zealous for the law, and they have been told about you that you teach all the Jews who are among the Gentiles to forsake Moses, telling them not to circumcise their children or observe the customs." (Acts 21:20–21)

Though the elders know the rumors are baseless, they propose a dramatic demonstration of Paul's fidelity to the law, a demonstration that will prove to those "zealous for the law" that Paul is no apostate (Acts 21:23–24). Based on Luke's account, there is no reason to regard Paul's willingness to comply as insincere. In fact, the rest of the story seems intent on demonstrating Paul's Jewish "orthodoxy."

Paul's arrest in Jerusalem is highly ironic. Jews who have followed Paul from Asia stir up the crowd:

> "Men of Israel, help! This is the man who is teaching men everywhere against the people and the law and this place; moreover he also brought Greeks into the temple, and he has defiled this holy place." (Acts 21:28)

The moment of his arrest, however, falls during Paul's purification at a time when he is participating in the holiest of vows (Acts 21:26). Paul, like Stephen, is charged with speaking against the temple and the law. The reader already knows the charges are completely without foundation.

The point is argued in detail in Paul's speeches given in his own defense. The speeches, which dominate the ensuing chapters, are very different from others in Acts. They are autobiographical to an extent unparalleled in Acts; twice Paul recounts the story of his conversion (Acts 22:6–16 and 26:9–18). The speeches seek not to convert but to prove Paul's innocence. And the charges against which Paul defends himself have nothing to do with matters of Roman law. The questions to which he addresses himself are posed in the charges leveled at him by fellow Jews: does Paul teach Jews to stop circumcision? does he preach against the law? is he an apostate? Paul's comments before the council and, later, before King Agrippa, are typical:

> "Brethren, I am a Pharisee, a son of Pharisees; with respect to the hope and the resurrection of the dead I am on trial." (Acts 23:6)

> "And now I stand here on trial for hope in the promise made by God to our fathers, to which our twelve tribes hope to attain, as they earnestly worship night and day." (Acts 26:6–7)

> "To this day I have had the help that comes from God, and so I stand here testifying to small and great, saying nothing but what the prophets and Moses said would come to pass." (Acts 26:22)

Though Paul's trial ostensibly deals with crimes against Roman law, the apologetic speeches deal with Paul's relationship to his Jewish tradition. To state it pointedly, the trial provides an opportunity to refute charges that Paul was a Jewish heretic. What is proved is that Paul could never have taught what his enemies charge him with teaching. He is, as he has always been, a faithful son of the covenant who believes that Jesus is the Christ.

As promised by God, Paul finally arrives in Rome—though not until he has experienced a series of extraordinary adventures. The most remarkable is a shipwreck, narrated in meticulous detail, surely one of the narrative masterpieces in the New Testament (Acts 27). The great missionary has his opportunity to testify in the imperial capital. He is not the first missionary; there is already a congregation in the city, though the author of Acts makes little of it (Acts 28:15–16). Significantly, in the final scene of his extraordinary career, Paul delivers one last address to a gathering of Jews in a synagogue. The reaction is typical: some believe, some do not. Paul concludes his testimony with a quotation from Isaiah and an ominous prediction:

> Let it be known to you then that this salvation of God has been sent to the Gentiles; they will listen." (Acts 28:29)

The story closes with Paul under house arrest, awaiting the disposition of his case, preaching during what we know will be his last days.

The concluding verses in Acts do not bring the story of the Jesus movement to a close. In fact, they anticipate a future in which as yet unnamed emissaries will carry the gospel to the ends of the earth, to Gentiles who "will listen." We must assume that the author and his audience live during that era of the Gentiles. Paul's appearance before the Jewish community in Rome does provide some sense of closure in the story, however. Paul has made such pronouncements earlier about salvation being sent to Gentiles when he encounters resistance at synagogues (Acts 13:46–47; 18:6). There is a note of finality here, however, suggesting that the epoch of the mission to the synagoguge, headed by Peter and Paul, is now past. The future of the movement lies with the Gentiles.

From Luke's perspective, Paul is probably the single most important Christian in the early church. Though by no means the only missionary, he seems to have had a greater impact on the Roman world than anyone. His churches dotted the map of Asia Minor and Greece. Paul was also controversial. His opponents included not only Sadducees who disliked his preaching of the resurrection but Jews from all over the empire who considered him a heretic. Even Jewish Christians were uneasy around Paul. The issue was Paul's understanding of the Torah and its relationship to faith in Christ. Luke's brief biography of Paul is more than a report; it is an apology, arguing that Paul was "orthodox" and belonged within the family of Jews who believed Jesus to be the Messiah. We might hazard a guess that what was at stake was not simply Paul and his personal reputation, but the status of that whole segment of Christendom that owed its existence to the great missionary. Perhaps what was at stake was the very unity of the church. That question, however, must await a later chapter.

CHAPTER IV

The Life of Faith

Luke's history of Jesus and of the spread of "the way" intends not simply to describe but also to prescribe. There are places where the author uses a direct approach: Jesus' parables about the misuse of wealth or about true neighborliness, his pronouncements on matters from Sabbath observance to fasting, and his comments about prayer offer glimpses not only of the good news Christian missionaries spread but of the life appropriate to those who confessed Jesus as Christ. The sermons of Peter and Stephen and Paul in Acts likewise speak about faith and discipleship.

Didactic interests are reflected in narratives as well, where teaching is more indirect. In Jesus' ministry and in the careers of his followers, readers are given a glimpse of what discipleship is like—what believers can expect from the world and what can be expected of them. Acts offers a picture of life lived as Jesus taught, related to the gospel as a full-grown plant to a seed. In fact, Jesus uses precisely this imagery to speak of his work (Luke 8:4–18; 13:18–19). Since Luke and Acts were written by the same author, it would be surprising if there were not some consistency in outlook.

It soon becomes apparent, however, that the seed/plant imagery for the Gospel and Acts is not totally adequate. Many seeds planted in the Gospel never germinate in Acts. And there are surprises. Possessions are not quite the problem for believers in Acts we might have expected from Mary's *Magnificat* or from Jesus' warnings. Jesus' followers seem less interested in outcasts than we might have anticipated. Scholars are perhaps correct in speaking of the limitations imposed on Luke by the gospel tradition he inherited.

What we see in Acts, perhaps, is how the author chose to interpret the tradition, selecting features particularly relevant to the situation of church as he viewed it.

In spite of differences, however, there is value in seeking a "Lukan" perspective on the life of faith in the Gospel and Acts. There are consistencies that afford a glimpse of a distinctive undertanding of discipleship.

Hospitality

Perhaps the most striking feature of Jesus' ministry in the Gospel of Luke is his concern for the outcast. When questioned about his association with the irreligious and the sick, Jesus responds by speaking about God. Finding the lost is what God wills above all else:

> "Just so, I tell you, there will be more joy in heaven over one sinner who repents than over ninety-nine righteous persons who need no repentance." (Luke 15:7)

Inclusion of repentant sinners within the kingdom of God is graphically illustrated in Jesus' ministry by their inclusion in table fellowship. Meals offered a special opportunity for intimacy and were governed by convention. Observant Jews understood the power of intimacy as a religious force and saw meals as an excellent opportunity to offer testimony to their tradition. Jesus' behavior scandalized them. Jesus understood the power of intimacy as well, but he intended to convey a different message. The meals he shared with his followers, he insisted, anticipated the fellowship to be shared when all would gather at table in the kingdom of God (Luke 22:30). The inclusiveness he embodied in his ministry offered a glimpse of the new reality his ministry heralded.

Meal scenes are frequent in Luke's Gospel, and the lessons taught are clear. When Levi, a tax collector, becomes a disciple, he gives a feast in Jesus' honor to which other sinners and tax collectors are invited. The Pharisees grumble. "I have not come to call the righteous, but sinners to repentance," Jesus responds (Luke 5:27–32). In reply to similar objections Jesus tells stories about a shepherd who leaves his flock in search of one stray (Luke 15:3–7), and a woman who leaves her work to find one lost coin (Luke 15:8–10). He tells of a profligate son who came to himself and returned home, to the joy of the father and the disgust of his older brother (Luke 15:11–32). The father's poignant question to his older son that ends the parable asks why the religious are unable to celebrate the return of sinners to the fold. Jesus, at least, is about the business of bringing strays back into the family. His concern is enacted in his table fellowship.

Table fellowship is important in Acts as well. Christians, we are told, attended the temple together and broke bread in their homes (Acts 2:46 and 20:7). There is a shift, however. Table fellowship is an important issue and the focus of debate, but the problem is not the inclusion of non-observant Jews. In Acts, the problem arises over the question of including Gentiles at table. As we have already noted, the conversion of Cornelius, the first Gentile convert, is a major event in Acts, marked by visions and apparitions and elaborate description. Peter becomes an unwitting evangelist to non-Jews. Upon his return from the home of Cornelius Peter is criticized by fellow Jews in Judea:

> So when Peter went up to Jerusalem, the circumcision party criticized him, saying, "Why did you go to uncircumcised men and eat with them?" (Acts 11:2–3)

The issue, as noted earlier, is not whether Gentiles are to be saved. It is whether or not they are to be included in table fellowship. Jewish law forbade such intercourse. Eating with Gentiles meant contamination for Jewish Christians.

This particular barrier to table fellowship was more difficult to break down than those Jesus encountered in his ministry, for the law itself erected the barrier. It is not surprising that the problem is not solved by an appeal to Jesus' practice. Jesus never transgressed the Torah in this regard. His dealings with Gentiles were always an exception (Luke 7:1–9). Luke respects the dilemma in which early Christians found themselves. On the one hand God is interested in welcoming repentant sinners; on the other he is the one who commanded circumcision and gave Moses the Torah. The problem is solved, but not by abrogating the law. God cleanses the Gentiles

through baptism (Acts 11:3–17), and James finds provisions within
the Torah that permit Gentiles to eat with Jews (Acts 15:19–21).

Barriers are broken down; Gentiles are included at meals and at
celebrations of the Lord's Supper. As in the Gospel, boundaries are
transgressed for the sake of enlarging the family. In Acts, however,
the significant barriers are those separating Jew and Gentile. Their
removal is cause for joy. The author of Acts would certainly agree
with the author of the letter to the Ephesians that table fellowship
between Jew and Gentile is nothing short of miraculous and an
expression of cosmic reconciliation (Eph. 2:11–22). The attention
the problem receives in Acts and the way the solution is presented
also reveal the author's profound empathy with Jewish Christians
who had to come to terms with an increasing number of Gentile
converts while still remaining faithful to their tradition.

The Problems and Possibilities of Possessions

Jesus' story is one of striking reversals. The one born to sit on the
throne of his father David and to reign over the house of Jacob
forever spends most of his career with the poor and the outcast. His
call, lifted from Isaiah, is to "preach good news to the poor" and to
"set at liberty those who are oppressed" (Luke 4:18). Eating with
sinners and healing the sick, Jesus fulfills his commission. His
overturning of established values in the name of the kingdom of
God aptly mirrors the will of God as Mary expresses it in her
Magnificat:

> "He has shown strength with his arm,
> he has scattered the proud in the imagination of their hearts,
> he has put down the mighty from their thrones,
> and exalted those of low degree;
> he has filled the hungry with good things,
> and the rich he has sent empty away." (Luke 1:51–53)

Acts, however, sketches a picture of a church that is neither poor
nor hungry. Twice the author comments about the pooling of
resources that eliminated need (Acts 2:44–45 and 4:34–37). Some,
like Joseph surnamed Barnabas, had property that they sold—im-

plying that they were relatively well off. The author comments that "the way" attracts several Gentiles of the nobility. Though believers in Acts display social consciousness, there is little evidence of a total social revolution under way, as the *Magnificat* might imply. Jesus' followers do not associate exclusively with the poor and the outcast.

Possessions are important both in Luke's Gospel and in Acts, however.[1] If the rich and mighty are not literally torn down from positions of power, they come in for special scrutiny. Wealth was not, for Jesus, a sign of God's approval. It was a danger. The story of the rich young man who could not part with his money (Luke 18:18–23), of the rich fool who invested only in transient possessions (Luke 12:15–21), and of the rich man and Lazarus who ended up in reversed roles in the afterlife (Luke 16:19–31) all portray possessions as a serious distraction—in some cases, as a genuine obstacle to discipleship.

The life of the church bears out Jesus' warnings. For some, wealth is an irresistible temptation that destroys life. Ananias and Sapphira, members of the Jerusalem congregation, were unable to part with their possessions (Acts 5:1–11). They sold their property for the church but held back some of the proceeds for themselves rather than turning the whole amount over to Peter. Their inability to part with their possessions was literally the cause of their undoing: both fell dead when confronted with their lie, providing for the whole church a dramatic illustration of Jesus' words, "For it is easier for a camel to go through the eye of a needle than for a rich man to enter the kingdom of God" (Luke 18:25).

Even in Luke's Gospel, Mary's statement about God's sending the rich empty away is somewhat modified during the course of the story. Though Jesus can pronounce woes on the rich and the full (Luke 6:24–25), he also on occasion redeems the wealthy. Zacchaeus the tax collector was "saved" (Luke 19:1–10), illustrating Jesus' desire to "seek and to save the lost." As a result, however, Zacchaeus gives half his wealth to the poor and repays fourfold any he defrauded. Crucial is the use of wealth.

The parable of the Good Samaritan likewise indicates that possessions can be used for good purposes (Luke 10:29–37). The story of the dishonest steward who used his position to make friends before he was fired issues a call to the righteous to be as prudent in their use of wealth as the "sons of this age" (Luke 16:1–9). The portrait of the early church emphasizes proper use of resources:

> And all who believed were together and had all things in common; and they sold their possessions and goods and distributed them to all, as any had need. (Acts 2:44–45)

> Now the company of those who believed were of one heart and soul, and no one said that any of the things which he possessed was his own, but they had everything in common. . . . There was not a needy person among them, for as many as were possessors of lands or houses sold them, and brought the proceeds of what was sold and laid it at the apostles' feet; and distribution was made to each as any had need. (Acts 4:32–35)

Possessions are important because they offer the possibility of generosity and charity. "Be merciful," Jesus told his followers, "even as your Father is merciful" (Luke 6:36). Pooling of resources allowed believers to fulfill his command.

The ideals were not unique to Luke nor even to the earliest Christians. Description of the first believers as being "of one heart and soul" and of having all things in common recalled ancient Greek definitions of friendship that enjoyed wide currency among philosophical groups in the Greek world of Luke's time.[2] The statements also recall Moses' prediction in Deuteronomy:

> But there will be no poor among you . . . if only you obey the voice of the LORD your God, being careful to do all this commandment which I command you this day. (Deut. 15:4–5)

Among the rabbis, the use of possessions for charitable purposes received high praise. A saying attributed to Rabbi Simeon the Just (300 B.C.E.?) expresses the importance of charity in this way:

> Simeon the Just was one of the remnants of the Great Synagogue. He used to say: By three things is the world sustained: by the Law, by the [Temple-] service, and by deeds of loving kindness. (*Aboth* 1:2)[3]

Such ideals, Luke insists, were embodied in the movement Jesus founded. "Sell your possessions, and give alms," Jesus advised his followers. According to Acts, they did. And when the author describes characters as pious, almost always he comments on their generosity. Peter and John, though they do not have silver or gold, give what they can to a poor beggar at the temple (Acts 3:2–6). Peter brings back to life a woman named Tabitha, who was "full of good works and acts of charity" (Acts 9:36). Cornelius, the first Gentile convert, is introduced as "a devout man who feared God with all his household, gave alms liberally to the people, and prayed constantly" (Acts 10:2; cf. 10:4, 31). In his defense before Felix, Paul describes his trip to Jerusalem as being for the purpose of bringing "to my nation alms and offerings" (Acts 24:17). Piety is closely linked with charity.

The Gospel as Luke conceives it has definite social implications. Early chapters promise surprises and reversals, and they occur. In Jesus' ministry, outcasts of all sorts are brought back into the family, including the poor. As the new community begins to take shape in Acts, however, it is not simply a collection of the exalted humble or the satisfied hungry. It continues to practice hospitality, but it is a community called to use its possessions wisely. Christians who have been shown mercy are invited to respond appropriately by doing merciful deeds. The author sees no clear separation of the sacred from the secular. Possessions, the most secular dimension of private life, are viewed as the clearest means by which to offer testimony to the faith. The story of the church illustrates the danger of wealth but also its enormous possibilities for good. Luke would have applauded the comment made centuries later by the Roman Emperor Julian (the Apostate) who was dismayed by the impact Christians were making on Roman society:

> It is disgraceful that when no Jew ever has to beg, and the impious Galileans [Christians] support not only their own poor but ours as well, all men see that our people lack aid from us.[4]

Life in the Spirit

Prior to the beginning of Jesus' ministry, John the Baptist predicted the coming of one mightier than he who "will baptize you with the Holy Spirit and with fire" (Luke 3:16). Before the promise is fulfilled, the Spirit is at work, but only sporadically. Zechariah and Elizabeth, Mary, Anna, and Simeon are moved by the Spirit to sing a song or to utter a prophecy. Jesus alone is the consistent bearer of the Spirit in the Gospel, "anointed" by the Spirit for his ministry (Luke 4:18). A new era begins with Pentecost when John's promise is fulfilled and the Holy Spirit is poured out on the disciples. The outpouring is to include "all flesh," according to Peter (Acts 2:17).

In light of the significance of the Spirit for the unfolding story in Acts, surprisingly little is said about the role of the Spirit in the life of the new community of faith. Three times the narrator notes that the coming of the Spirit resulted in speaking in tongues: Acts 2:4; 10:46; and 19:6. Once the result is that believers "spoke the word of God with boldness" (Acts 4:31). Little more is said than that the coming of the Spirit had obvious results.

We know from several chapters in Paul's first letter to the church at Corinth that the presence of the Spirit at worship, evidenced by various forms of inspired speech, was an important element in the experience of the young church. Manifestations of the Spirit included both articulate speech, which Paul terms "prophecy," and inarticulate speech requiring translation (1 Cor. 14:1–5), which Paul refers to as "tongues." When Paul lists various manifestations of the Spirit, only apostles rank higher than prophets in terms of respect (1 Cor. 12:28). The immense authority accorded Christian prophets in the later writing known as the *Didache*—even when some were known frauds—testifies to the scope of charismatic authority in Christian circles (*Didache* 11). Managing such authority provided second-century believers with their greatest conflict, nearly destroying the Christian movement.[5] The experience of Corinthian Christians already anticipated the conflict. Dramatic manifestations of the Spirit were difficult for the church to manage and, as in Corinth in the first century, led to schism. Given the apparent prominence of such manifestations of the Spirit and their importance within community structure, the sparse references to the work of the Spirit within the ordinary life of believers in Acts is the more striking.

Such omissions perhaps offer clues to the purpose of Acts. The author seems more interested in breadth than depth. The narrative traces the sweep of the new movement across the face of the Roman world. The Spirit is the motive power in the story. Not surprisingly, therefore, the author focuses attention on the larger story. The Spirit inspires the witnesses who bring the message of repentance and forgiveness (Luke 24:47–49; Acts 1:8; 2:1–10; 4:8–12). The Spirit instructs messengers where to go and even what to say (Acts 8:29, 39; 10:19–20; 16:6). Even references to speaking in tongues serve to mark important transitions in the mission. Pentecost marks the beginning. The mission in Samaria is legitimized when Peter and John lay hands on the Samaritans and they receive the Spirit (Acts 8:17). In chapter 10, God interrupts Peter's sermon by pouring out the Spirit on Cornelius and his household, thus cleansing the Gentiles, fitting them for participation at worship and at meals. Finally, in chapter 19 Paul demonstrates the superiority of baptism in Jesus' name to the baptism of John when believers in Ephesus receive the gift of tongues.

For Luke, the Holy Spirit was important principally as the driving force behind the new movement inaugurated at Pentecost. He spends little time describing in detail the place of charismatic gifts in congregations. We can observe that inspired speech was viewed by believers as a clear sign of a new power at work in the world and as the sign that a new era had begun. Acts also suggests that the inclusion of Gentiles in Jewish Christian worship occurred in the context of charismatic experiences. The narrative offers little detail, however. Though Peter's speech envisions all believers as recipients of the Spirit, it is the impact of the Spirit on principal characters that interested Luke. Though the author hints that manifestations of the Spirit were an important ingredient in the life of faith, he focuses his attention on movements of history. It is in this larger sense that Acts may be termed the story of the Holy Spirit.

Openness to the Future

Discipleship can be described by attending to details, like attitudes toward possessions or strangers. It must also include offering some sense of the world, more difficult to specify but nonetheless real: what is it like out there where the life of faith will be lived? what are our prospects? will we find the world hospitable? Luke's narrative provides answers to such questions, even if he writes about larger-than-life heroes who are not simply paradigmatic believers. Like any artist, he offers a glimpse of what life is really like. Even exaggerations and distortions call attention to aspects of reality easily overlooked. Attentive readers learn something about attitudes toward the world and the future as well as about generosity and hospitality.

Perhaps the first impression we receive is that the world is an inhospitable place. It ignores the birth of the child born to be king, and when it becomes aware of his presence, the trouble begins. Jesus' first sermon at Nazareth nearly gets him killed. John the Baptist, his cousin who prepares the way, meets a violent death at the hands of established powers. Jesus' death at the hands of Roman officials comes as no surprise. During his temptation, Satan speaks of all political power as his. Referring to the "kingdoms of the world," he tells Jesus:

> "To you I will give all this authority and their glory; for it has been delivered to me, and I give it to whom I will." (Luke 4:6)

Jesus' refusal to compromise makes confrontation with the kingdoms of the world inevitable. Jesus expects trouble, and so should his followers:

> "But before all this they will lay their hands on you and persecute you, delivering you up to the synagogues and prisons, and you will be brought before kings and governors for my name's sake. . . . You will be delivered up even by parents and brothers and kinsmen and friends, and some of you they will put to death; you will be hated by all for my name's sake." (Luke 21:12–17)

Acts bears out his grim predictions. Stephen is martyred, as is James the brother of John. Peter and John are in constant trouble with the Jewish authorities in Jerusalem, in and out of prison. Paul is in trouble from the outset. In fact, Ananias is told that the Lord will show Paul "how much he must suffer for the sake of my name"

(Acts 9:16)—almost the theme of Paul's career. Even if Acts ends before Paul's trial concludes, there can be no doubt about the outcome.

The message of Jesus and his followers in Luke-Acts is not world-affirming. The message is about repentance. Conflict that arises is interpreted by appeal to the experience of Israel's prophets who were persecuted for speaking the truth. The story Luke recounts is about conflict, from the mythic level to the social. Jesus speaks of his ministry as casting fire upon the earth (Luke 12:49). Believers must expect trouble from established powers, family quarrels, even outright persecution in the service of the crucified and risen King.

Yet the story Luke tells is also about possibilities—possibilities understood not simply in other-worldly terms. To a far greater extent than anywhere else in the New Testament, Luke-Acts pictures the world as a hopeful place. At one end of the spectrum stands the Gospel of John. John's world is painted in blacks and whites; there are no grays. His world is totally polarized. Those few who are of the truth hear and understand; others are blind and deaf, incapable of insight or faith. The supposed children of God prefer darkness to light "because their deeds were evil" (John 3:19). When God's Word comes into the world God created, God's own people do not receive God (John 1:11).

Luke's world is a different place. There are vivid colors, genuine personalities. Society is not polarized. Some are hostile to Jesus, others are genuinely open; some are indifferent, undecided, but not hostile. Felix, for example, is corrupt and weak, but he is mildly interested in what Paul has to say about Jesus (Acts 24:24–26). Festus and Agrippa gave Paul a hearing, even if what he says about the resurrection strikes them as madness (Acts 25:13—26:32). Many are ready to listen. Crowds flock to Jesus—and also to his followers. Peter's sermons convert thousands. Paul makes a believer even out of his jailer. There are hostile responses—but there are many more who are ready to listen to the gospel and to be persuaded.

Despite opposition, the new movement is an enormous success. Three thousand are baptized at Pentecost. By the time of Paul's visit to Jerusalem in chapter 21, Jerusalem elders can report that tens of thousands of pious Jews have come to faith in Jesus (Acts 21:20). The point is scored not only by numbers but by vivid accounts of successes—frequently at the expense of competitors. Philip performs mighty works greater than those of the renowned Simon Magus (Simon the Magician[6]) (Acts 8:9–13). Paul blinds Elymas the magician, thus making a believer out of the proconsul Sergius Paulus (Acts 13:6–12). Later he silences the spirit in a young woman, getting himself into trouble with her owners (Acts 16:16–24). So impressed are crowds with Paul and Barnabas that they hail them as gods (Acts 14:8–18). Those Paul converted at Ephesus burned their books of magic—worth fifty thousand pieces of silver, the narrator comments (Acts 19:19). There is power in Jesus' name. The frequent competitions in Acts permit some glimpse of that power in comparative terms.

If people are impressed with power, they are also open to persuasion. Speeches given by Peter and Paul make an impact. Thousands believe, even some priests (Acts 6:7). Common people respond, but so do members of the nobility (Acts 17:12). Missionaries argue from the Scriptures, finding a ready audience at every synagogue. Some do not believe and stir up trouble, but many are persuaded. Even the sophisticated Athenians grant Paul a hearing on the famed Areopagus (Acts 17:16–31). The rare opportunity yields fruit (Acts 17:32–34).

The world Luke sketches is an open place. Matters of faith can be debated, arguments offered, opponents refuted. Real conversation is possible. Speakers arguing from the Scriptures can assume that some common ground exists even with unbelievers.[7] By contrast, John's Gospel envisions no common ground shared by believers and unbelievers. One is either a child of light or a child of darkness. Those God has taught respond; those he has not do not (John 5, 8).

In theological terms, God's mode of involvement in the world is not as hidden as in other Gospels. Followers of Jesus are public figures whose power and eloquence are visible to all. Their enemies have no power to match theirs, no arguments with which to refute the claims on Jesus' behalf. Opponents of the apostles can only seek to silence them. So obvious is God's truth, so confident is the author of the outcome of the new movement that he is willing to let history decide the truth of Christian claims. Ironically, it is Gamaliel, a renowned member of the high court—one of the enemy—who enunciates the criterion by which to measure truth:

> So in the present case I tell you, keep away from these men and let them alone; for if this plan or this undertaking is of men, it will fail; but if it is of God, you will not be able to overthrow them. You might even be found opposing God! (Acts 5:38–39)

The narrative bears out his thesis. Imprisonments result in miraculous deliverance, fulfilling Jesus' prediction, "Not a hair of your head shall perish" (Luke 21:18). Even the martyrdom of Stephen, an exception to the rule, serves only to further the mission. The expulsion of the Hellenists after Stephen's death drives them into new territory where the gospel can be preached. Philip evangelizes the Samaritans. Other Hellenists, driven to Antioch, found a church where Gentiles come to share in the gospel, a church that eventually commissions Paul as a missionary (Acts 11:19–26).

Paul's career is itself testimony to the irresistible power of God at work among the faithful. Though Paul suffers as a missionary, nothing halts his progress. He escapes from prison after converting the jailer; he recovers from stonings and beatings, escapes plots against his life; though adrift at sea for days and eventually shipwrecked, he arrives in Rome—as God had promised (Acts 27). Even when bitten by a poisonous serpent, Paul is unharmed (Acts 28:4–6). Providence is at work, visible for all to see—at least to those not committed in advance to falsehood. The reader of Luke-Acts cannot help but sense the optimism that permeates its pages.

This feature of the narrative has elicited comment from many interpreters. Paul's own writings set in vivid relief Luke's tendency to play down conflict and to portray the church as harmonious. Paul's reflection on his sufferings in his letters reveals an understanding of life and faith far more profound than Luke's own. Not surprisingly, the adequacy of Luke's view of the world has been hotly debated. Many of the arguments about Luke-Acts are thinly

veiled attacks on religious or philosophical views in present society
interpreters believe to be inadequate.[8] To paraphrase the famous
dictum of Julius Wellhausen, commentaries are often as instructive
about the nature of the commentator as about the material they
seek to explicate.

A recent book by David Tiede has attempted to reformulate the
question about the adequacy of Luke's view of the world by locating
Luke-Acts more precisely in its historical setting.[9] Modern readers,
he argues, easily miss the pain and anguish that preceded the writing
of Luke-Acts. Interpreters view the volumes as establishment
literature, written to offer justification for a new and dominant
religious institution. In fact, Tiede argues, the volumes must be
understood as inner-Jewish attempts to come to terms with the
devastation resulting from the wars against Rome and the
destruction of Jerusalem. Those who believed in Jesus were caught
in the devastation themselves, torn apart socially. Questions about
the will of God and election were raised in the face of historical
events that seemed to undermine any confidence in God or in the
future. In such a setting, the two-volume work would have had a
rather different function than normally assumed and would sound
different.

The matter need not be settled in this chapter, though it should
already be apparent that I tend to agree with Tiede. Here we need
simply note that within the spectrum of New Testament authors,
Luke tends to be the most optimistic. The world in which faith is to
be lived out is open and accessible, the future one of limitless
possibility.

CHAPTER V

The People of God

"But you shall receive power when the Holy Spirit has come upon you; and you shall be my witnesses in Jerusalem and in all Judea and Samaria and to the end of the earth." (Acts 1:8)

The story that begins with a simple country priest in the Jerusalem temple ends with the great apostle Paul in the imperial capital, preaching and teaching about the Lord Jesus Christ "openly and unhindered" (Acts 28:31). Luke tells of a movement that spreads like wildfire from its humble origins, a movement whose progress cannot be impeded. Little wonder that commentators have customarily spoken of Luke-Acts as the New Testament writings most interested in tracing the spread of the gospel to all peoples, i.e., to Gentiles. In speaking of Luke's Gospel, the Oxford Study Bible refers to the "universal mission of Jesus," meaning a mission intended not only for Jews. Werner Georg Kümmel, in his *Introduction to the New Testament,* derives from the geographical spread of the gospel a whole view of history:

> From most of these answers it follows that the geographical organization of the account in Acts in the sense of a broadening of mission territory includes the gradual broadening of subject matter: from the preaching to the Jews in Jerusalem to the final self-exclusion of the Jews from God's salvation and to the unhindered proclamation before the Gentiles in Rome.[1]

Howard Kee is more concise in his *Understanding the New Testament:*

> Luke is content to lay stress on the shift of focus of the Gospel from the Jew to the Gentile.[2]

The view accords well with the traditional ascription of the two volumes to "Luke the beloved physician" (Col. 4:14), a Gentile Christian who traveled with Paul. It would seem reasonable that a Gentile who traveled with the famous apostle to the Gentiles should undertake a history of the Gentile mission, tracing the story as far as the imperial capital.

Scholars who reject traditional authorship of Luke-Acts still concur in their reading of the place of Jews in the plan of the work. Scholars like Ernst Haenchen and Hans Conzelmann, for example, believe that the author was not a companion of Paul but an anonymous Christian who sought to provide for a generation of believers that no longer anticipated the immediate return of Christ a secure place in the world. New ecclesiastical institutions required justification, and relations to existing political powers needed clarification. The author of the two volumes also sought, they argue, to clarify the relationship between Christians and Jews. Conzelmann's views are typical:

> It is plain that the debate concerning the Jewish cultus does not belong to the present, but is a matter of history. It is set out by means of historical reflection on the "beginning" of the community, not in an actual struggle concerning the present relationship of the Church to the Temple and the Law. The solution—freedom from the Law and the Temple—is already before Luke as an accomplished fact. Thus Luke is the first writer who deliberately describes the past of the community as "the past."[3]

The church, in other words, understands itself as distinct from the synagogue. The author does not deny that the Christian movement has roots in Judaism, but he seeks to relegate all vestiges of such piety to the past. Luke-Acts, the argument goes, sees the church as belonging to a new era.

Recently, significant challenges to this traditional reading of Luke-Acts have appeared, resulting in large measure from revisions in our picture of the first century. What began as a trickle of essays has become a steady stream of articles and monographs.[4] From various angles, scholars have argued that the two volumes belong not outside the Jewish tradition, but within; that the author was more concerned to argue for continuity with Israel's heritage than discontinuity; that there is no theology of "replacement" whereby the church supercedes Israel in God's plan of salvation; that Luke-Acts by no means considers adherence to the Torah as past and that it is anachronistic even to speak of a "Christian church" as a new, self-conscious religious movement alongside Judaism.

In this chapter we will examine in finer detail what we have touched on throughout the volume—the relationship that exists between Israel and believers in Jesus. We will examine the issue by focusing on the crucial category, "the People of God."

Piety and the Law

With few exceptions, the characters in Luke's story are Jews. That is hardly surprising. More significant is the author's interest in their Jewishness. The first characters we meet are introduced as pious—a piety measure by Jewish standards:

> And they were both righteous before God, walking in all the commandments and ordinances of the Lord blameless. (Luke 1:6)

Of the evangelists, only Luke observes that John's parents had their son circumcised on the eighth day. Jesus too is circumcised in accordance with the commandment. Luke tells of the visit by Jesus' parents to the temple "for their purification according to the law of Moses" (Luke 2:22), noting somewhat redundantly that Joseph and Mary returned home only "when they had performed everything according to the law of the Lord" (Luke 2:39). Their journey to Jerusalem for Passover when Jesus was twelve, another story unique to Luke, accords fully with expectations of observant Jews.

Some have argued that the opening two chapters in the Gospel of Luke are singular in this respect, displaying an interest in Jewish piety uncommon elsewhere in the Gospel or Acts.[5] Such arguments cannot be sustained. Luke's Jesus is even more scrupulous about aspects of the law than Matthew's. Jesus, for example, has virtually no dealings with Gentiles in the Gospel of Luke. Luke tells no story about Jesus' meeting with a Gentile woman from Phoenecia, as do Matthew and Mark (Mark 7:24–30; Matt. 15:21–28). In fact, Luke seems to avoid the suggestion that Jesus even traveled in Gentile territory.[6] Luke knows, as Peter comments to Cornelius in Acts, that the law forbids contacts between Jews and Gentiles (Acts 10:28). In Luke, Jesus shows no inclination in his ministry to transgress the law in this respect.

One exception is the story of Jesus' healing of a Roman centurion's servant (Luke 7:1–10). In Matthew's version of the same story, the Gentile comes to Jesus and personally asks for help (Matt. 8:5–13). In Luke, elders of the Jews intercede for the soldier:

> When he heard of Jesus, he sent to him elders of the Jews, asking him to come and heal his slave. And when they came to Jesus, they besought him earnestly, saying, "He is worthy to have you do this for him, for he loves our nation, and he built us our synagogue." (Luke 7:3–5)

Jesus never does deal directly with the Roman in Luke's story.

The situation does not change in Acts. The first believers are depicted as scrupulous observers of the law, attending the temple regularly (Acts 2:46; 3:1; 5:12). The thousands "among the Jews of those who have believed" in Jerusalem are all "zealous for the law" (Acts 21:20). Even Paul, whose alleged liberal view of the tradition is a matter of some concern to the elders, characterizes himself as a pious Jew who would never utter a word against the Scriptures or the tradition. Paul's own piety, at least in Acts, is defined by the Torah.

One of the major themes in Luke-Acts is the extension of salvation to the Gentiles. Preparation is made early in the Gospel and in Jesus' thematic statements in Luke 24 and Acts 1. With considerable formality, Acts recounts the conversion and admission of the first Gentiles in the story of Peter and Cornelius. No story more clearly reflects an appreciation for the Jewish law, however. Rather than inaugurating an era when obedience to the Torah ceases, the account provides an occasion for accommodating Gentiles within the family of faith without in any way abrogating the Torah as a structure for the life of the community.

Significantly it is Peter who presides at the conversion of the first Gentile. Luke had other options. He might have followed the career of the Hellenists driven out of Jersualem (Acts 8:1). He tells of the work of Philip among the Samaritans but returns only later to those who settled in Antioch and worked among Gentiles (Acts 11:19–26). The author might have followed the career of Paul a bit further. We read of his conversion in chapter 9, but his career as a missionary begins only after a lengthy interruption in the narrative (Acts 10:32—12:24). When Paul's story resumes, we learn about his work among Gentiles. Perhaps it is important to Luke that the "liberal" Hellenists and Paul, whose attitude toward the law is questionable, are not the initiators of the Gentile mission. No one could question Peter's credentials as a Jew.[7]

Visions and apparitions initiate this new departure in Acts, underscoring its importance. The first visit to Gentiles occurs not because of Peter but in spite of him. He has three visions at lunchtime dealing with attitudes toward ritual purity (Acts 10:9–16), providing Peter an opportunity to affirm his own respect for purity: "No, Lord; for I have never eaten anything that is common or unclean" (Acts 10:14). The vision speaks not of abrogating rules but of cleansing: "What God has cleansed, you must not call common" (Acts 10:15). By pouring out the Spirit on Gentiles later in the narrative, God cleanses them—at least that is the imagery used in Acts.

While Peter is having a vision, messengers are already on their way to him—sent by Cornelius in response to the instructions of an angel who appeared to him the day before (Acts 10:3–8). Cornelius, the first Gentile convert in Acts, is hardly a typical Gentile. Luke describes him as "a devout man who feared God with all his household, gave alms liberally to the people, and prayed constantly to God" (Acts 10:2). Cornelius does all that is expected of a pious Jew. He is a Gentile only in that he is uncircumcised.

Even so, Peter is hesitant about visiting his home. He explains to Cornelius that he came only because God instructed him to do so:

> "You yourselves know how unlawful it is for a Jew to associate with or to visit any one of another nation; but God has shown me that I should not call any man common or unclean." (Acts 10:28)

Despite the elaborate preparations, in spite of his visions and new-found insight, Peter is astounded—as are his Jewish companions—when the Holy Spirit is poured out on Cornelius and his household (Acts 10:44–48).

The baptism of Cornelius and his household stirs up controversy when Peter returns to Jerusalem. The "circumcision party" criticizes Peter—not because he baptized Gentiles but because he ate with them (Acts 11:1–3). In their minds, the issue is not whether Gentiles will be saved but under what circumstances. The problem is the law: the Torah forbids social intercourse with non-Jews. When Peter recounts the Cornelius affair, he does not suggest that the rules have been set aside but that God has "cleansed" the Gentiles, thus fitting them for participation at meals with Jews.

The formal conclusion of the matter comes only with the so-called Apostolic Conference in Acts 15. Some Judean Christians are still not convinced about the status of the Gentiles. Paul, Barnabas, and the church at Antioch seem to be at the center of the controversy. A delegation is sent to Jerusalem to resolve the matter. It is difficult to imagine that the conference described in Acts 15 is the same one Paul discusses in Galatians 2. In Acts, Paul plays no role in the actual decision making. Peter and James are the principals. Peter tells the story of Cornelius once more, and James[8]—someone to whom we have not yet been introduced—issues a decree. Quoting from Amos, James lays down the following guidelines for dealing with Gentiles in a letter to be carried throughout the church:

> Therefore my judgment is that we should not trouble those of the Gentiles who turn to God, but should write to them to abstain from pollutions of idols and from unchastity and from what is strangled and from blood. (Acts 15:19–20)

The formal decree does not provide Gentiles with complete freedom from the Torah. It imposes on them the obligations traditionally imposed on "sojourners" within Israel, non-Jews who sought to live with Jews without undergoing circumcision (see Lev. 16—17).[9] The problem—prohibition of social intercourse with non-Jews in the Torah—is solved by appeal to the Torah, thus in a thoroughly Jewish manner. Gentiles who come to faith in Jesus must keep kosher if they are to eat with Jewish Christians. The

Apostolic Decree testifies to the continuing validity of the law as a guide to life for both Jews and Gentiles.

In Acts as in the opening chapters of the Gospel of Luke, piety is defined by the Torah. Nowhere does Luke suggest—as Paul does in his letters—that believing in Jesus means the abrogation of the Torah. Even Gentiles are obliged to keep that portion of the Torah appropriate to them as non-Jews. Conzelmann's views stated at the beginning of the chapter are thus incorrect. The law remains intact within the church. The people of God in the Gospel and in Acts are primarily children of Abraham who live by the law. The only exception made for non-Jews is that they do not require circumcision to live within the family. Like the thousands of Jewish believers in Jerusalem who are zealous for the law, the whole church lives in observance of the commandments.

The Law and Israel

Christian readers of the New Testament have always had some difficulty understanding the place of the law in Judaism. Part of the difficulty has been a Protestant misreading of the Torah according to which law and legalism are equivalent. Numerous scholars from George Foote Moore to Hans Joachim Schoeps to E. P. Sanders have argued against such a reading of Torah piety.[10] In the most recent such study to appear, *Paul and Palestinian Judaism,* Ed Sanders demonstrates that in Judaism the Torah was never a means of winning favor in God's eyes, that Jews as well as Christians understood God as gracious and forgiving. The clarity of his argument and the massive documentation should set such classical misunderstandings to rest once and for all.

Such clarification is helpful for reading Luke-Acts. Luke views the law of Moses as central to the life of believers in Jesus, but not as a means to salvation. In fact, the law in Luke-Acts has little to do with salvation. It is primarily a sign of identity, the mark that distinguishes the people of God from other peoples in the world.

The law as a mark of identity had been a feature of Judaism long before Luke. Particularly for Jews living outside Israel among Gentiles, it was adherence to a distinctive code that identified a member of God's elect. Ceremonial rules were as important as ethical, for it was precisely the visible signs of obedience to the law—like abstaining from pork, resting on Saturday, and practicing circumcision—that kept Jewishness visible in a Gentile world. When other signs of identity perished—a land, a king, and a temple—adherence to the Torah held the community together. The Torah served as a pointer to the one true God in a world full of idols; it identified those who lived by it as worshipers of that God.

Luke shared that view of the law. His narrative assumes that if there is a people of God, they will live by the law. Zechariah and Elizabeth, Joseph and Mary, Jesus, Peter, and Paul are all portrayed as observant Jews. Criticisms from other Jews are answered from within the tradition. The most sensitive matters, like eating with Gentiles, are justified by appeal to the Scriptures (Acts 15). As Luke tells the story of Jesus and his followers, nothing could justify a charge that the movement is an attack on the law. It is the enemies of the Christ who break the law (Acts 7:51–53).

Paul's attitude toward the law is of special concern to the author. The elders in Jerusalem acknowledge that Paul's reputation is suspect among Jews:

> "and they have been told about you that you teach all the Jews who are among the Gentiles to forsake Moses, telling them not to circumcise their children or observe the customs." (Acts 21:21)

Paul willingly agrees to the elaborate demonstration of faithfulness to the law the elders propose (Acts 21:23–24), since, as he insists later, he never did anything "against the people or the customs of our fathers" (Acts 28:17). The Jerusalem elders know that Paul has lived in observance of the law (Acts 21:24).

The author of Luke-Acts has a different view of the law from Paul himself; he solved the Jew-Gentile problem differently from the great apostle to the Gentiles.[11] There had been in his view no fundamental change in the structure of the Jewish faith since the coming of the Messiah. Luke could never have said, as Paul did, that "Christ is the end of the law" (Rom. 10:4). The issue for Luke was not how one was to be saved but whether the saved could lay claim to Israel's heritage. Since Abraham, God's people had practiced circumcision as a sign of their election. In Luke's view that had not changed. Israel's Messiah had come and a new era in the history of God's people had dawned. Gentiles had been included in the family, but there still existed for Luke only one Israel, one people of God faithful to the law, one history of salvation begun with the call of Abraham. For him, Israel's law was the sign of continuity.

A Family Divided

Luke-Acts is not about the birth of a new religion. The term "Christian," used only twice in Acts (and three times in the entire New Testament), is employed by pagans to identify believers in Jesus ("messianists" is the term that would have been used by Jews). The author speaks of the new movement as "the way" or as a "sect." Nor is the expression "new Israel" ever used to speak of the new group of believers. From Luke's perspective, there is only one Israel, and his story recounts the latest chapter in the history of that people.

The most recent chapter of Israel's history is not harmonious, however. It is marked by deep division within the family. That division was anticipated from the outset. Simeon predicted that Jesus was "set for the fall and rising of many in Israel" (Luke 2:33), and his promise is fulfilled in Acts. Opposition to Jesus, which culminates in his crucifixion, continues as opposition to those who preach repentance and forgiveness in his name. Though the preaching of Peter in Jerusalem achieves extraordinary success, there is also opposition: the authorities seek to silence the missionaries (Acts 4—5); Stephen is executed; Paul is arrested, barely escaping death at the hands of Jews sworn to destroy him.

Luke seeks not simply to record the division within Israel; he offers an interpretation. Peter's speech in Acts 3 provides a framework within which opposition can be understood. In the second half of the speech, Peter quotes Deuteronomy 18, with some embellishment from Leviticus:

> "Moses said, 'The Lord God will raise up for you a prophet from your brethren as he raised me up. You shall listen to him in whatever he tells you. And it shall be that every soul that does not listen to that prophet shall be destroyed from the people.' " (Acts 3:22–23)

The offer of salvation in Jesus' name, understood in terms of Joel's prophecy in Peter's previous speech, is cast in a different light here. As the prophet-like Moses, Jesus offers Israelites a choice. As in Deuteronomy, they must choose: those who obey his word demonstrate their allegiance to God; those who refuse his word deny their birthright. Those who do not heed Jesus' words exclude themselves from Israel. The opening scenes in Acts thus describe a purge. Jews are offered the opportunity to affirm their heritage by accepting the testimony of the apostles. Those who accept the offer of salvation in Jesus' name remain true Jews. Those who refuse the offer may no longer be regarded as Jews.

The theme of division within the family of Israel also figures prominently in Stephen's speech, as we noted earlier. From the time of the patriarchs—Israel's sons—members of the family opposed God's chosen. Joseph, Moses, and "all the prophets" were persecuted by false brethren within Israel. Internal division is nothing new. Those who rejected Jesus and brought Stephen to trial are cast as descendents of ancestors who consistently opposed those on whom God had set the Spirit.

It is noteworthy that opposition to the apostles comes principally from Sadducees—the aristocratic leaders of the temple. Elsewhere in Acts we learn that Sadducees "say that there is no resurrection, nor angel, nor spirit" (Acts 23:8). Their opposition to Jesus, Peter, Stephen, and Paul arises from their refusal to accept resurrection as a possibility and their inability to see beyond the centrality of the temple. The destruction of the temple by Roman legions, a memory by the time Luke wrote the Acts of the Apostles, offered compelling evidence to followers of the Messiah that it was the messianists and not their opponents who deserved the name "Israelites."

The division within Israel dominates even the career of Paul. Paul's preaching in synagogues across the face of the Roman Empire creates enclaves of "true" Jews, but it also stirs up opposition. Angry Jews hound Paul wherever he goes, succeeding finally in securing his arrest in Jerusalem (Acts 21:27–30). Once again, interpretation of such opposition is crucial. In his opening address in the synagogue at Antioch of Pisidia, Paul concludes with a quotation from Habakkuk, noted earlier (Acts 13:40–41).

Habakkuk's prophecy is fulfilled—tragically. Jews scoff at Paul; we know they will perish.

The problem of opposition to Jesus and his followers from within Israel lies close to the heart of Luke-Acts. The depth of the problem is reflected in the attention Luke devotes to it. How could God's elect refuse the offer of forgiveness and life in Jesus' name? Why could they not see the truth so clearly set before them? Luke, like other New Testament authors, had finally to resort to Israel's Scriptures for answers to such difficult and painful questions. It is hardly accidental that the concluding scene in Acts offers a final glimpse of a divided people of God—and a final interpretation of that division:

> So, as they disagreed among themselves, they departed, after Paul had made one statement: "The Holy Spirit was right in saying to your fathers through Isaiah the prophet:
> 'Go to this people and say,
> You shall indeed hear but never understand,
> and you shall indeed see but never perceive.
> For this people's heart has grown dull,
> and their ears are heavy of hearing,
> and their eyes they have closed;
> lest they should perceive with their eyes,
> and hear with their ears,
> and understand with their heart,
> and turn for me to heal them.'
> Let it be known to you then that this salvation of God has been sent to the Gentiles; they will listen." (Acts 28:25–29)

Though some scholars argue that Acts ends with some hope for Jews who have not yet accepted the gospel of the risen Christ, it is difficult not to sense that with the ending of Acts an era is over. The restoration of Israel, accomplished in fulfillment of God's promises, has now been completed. Unbelieving Jews have been "destroyed from the people." The tragic division within Israel has been accomplished—as God promised it would be. The future of Israel lies with the Gentiles: they will listen.

The dawning of the "time of the Gentiles" does not imply, however, the demise of the old Israel. The people of God have a future only because they have a past and a present, only because of those circumcised believers whose presence guarantees historical continuity. Even if no longer numerically superior at the time Luke wrote, those Jewish Christians served an essential function in Luke's history. Their presence was visible testimony that God had been truthful to the people, that the promises made to Abraham had indeed been fulfilled. We might even say that for Luke, without believers from among the circumcised the church had no right to claim Israel's heritage as its own. Only thus could the church apply to itself the designation, People of God.

CHAPTER VI

"So That You May Know How Well-founded Are the Things You Have Been Taught"

Both the difficulty and the fascination of biblical studies arise from the paucity of data about the biblical documents and their background. If the New Testament or sources contemporary with it provided solid information about authors and the circumstances under which they wrote, few scholarly works would be required. Because information is sketchy, many theories are possible and the corpus of secondary literature vast. Further, what information we possess about the first century is vulnerable to new discoveries. In recent decades, archaeological data and literary remains, the Dead Sea Scrolls in particular, have blown enormous holes in our theories about Judaism in the first century of the common era. The history of the period is being drastically revised, and though an outline is taking shape, scholarly concensus is years away.[1]

Such historical information is of critical importance to students of the New Testament. Our reading of any literature depends upon the background against which the narratives or letters must be interpreted. Books, like words, derive their meaning from a context. As our interpretation of the context changes, so too does our understanding of the books.

For decades, biblical scholars operated with a picture of early Christianity dominated by the work of Johannes Weiss and Albert Schweitzer, whose reading of Christian literature was in turn dependent upon a view of first-century Judaism that now seems oversimplified. Jesus' career, they argued, made sense only against the background of apocalyptic—intense speculation about the end times fueled by political unrest in Roman-occupied Palestine. Against this background, Jesus announced the nearness—the temporal proximity—of the kingdom of God whose rule was expected to break into time, bringing history to a close. Schweitzer in particular argued that *the* problem faced by preachers and teachers in the early church was the failure of Jesus' expectations to be realized. He did not return on the clouds of heaven; the kingdom in all its splendor did not arrive. The task for theologians, Schweitzer argued, was to make sense of this one disquieting reality: why had Jesus not returned? had his followers misunderstood? were they—was Jesus—wrong? what were the faithful to expect from the future?

Despite the considerable body of data about the first century unearthed since Schweitzer, many Lukan scholars have interpreted Luke-Acts against the background Schweitzer sketched. Luke, they argued, faced the problem of Jesus' failure to return and history to end. He wrote to prepare believers for the long haul and to carve out a place for the church in the world. There are many variations of the basic theme. Some, like G. Klein, view Acts as an attempt to justify emerging ecclesiastical offices, with the twelve apostles as representatives of a college of bishops.[2] Others argue that to survive in the Roman world, Christians would have required permission from the Roman government to worship. Luke, they reason, sought to make the case that Christianity was politically harmless and that it deserved imperial protection.[3] Hans Conzelmann argues that Luke sought to consolidate the place of the church in the world by providing it with an ideological base, a history of salvation which both provided some sense of rootedness and accounted for the differences between his own time and the early days of the movement. A major task, Conzelmann believes, was to explain the transition from a Jewish church to a Gentile movement, free from the law. Luke sought to meet the needs of third-generation Christians.[4]

The interpretation of Luke-Acts offered in this volume, which is heavily dependent upon the work of Nils Dahl and Jacob Jervell, moves in a different direction. The problem of time—Jesus' failure to return—no longer appears as the motive force behind the composition of the two volumes. The delay of the parousia seems to have been far less critical during the last decades of the first century than relations within the Jewish community and relations between Jews and their non-Jewish neighbors. At the center of Luke's work stands a constellation of images that cannot be derived from a concern about the end of time—matters relating to the Torah and the temple, to Gentiles and table fellowship, to relations between Jews who believed in Jesus and those who did not. Recent historical studies have had their most significant impact at this point. Previously, scholars assumed that with the destruction of the temple in 70 c.e., Jewish Christianity ceased to be of any significance and the Christian movement became completely Gentile oriented. That assumption is being challenged on numerous fronts.

The impact of the interpretive shift has been apparent in Matthean and Johannine studies in the last decade. Raymond Brown and J. Louis Martyn have argued convincingly that the Gospel of John was written for Jewish Christians who had been excluded from the synagogue.[5] Unwilling to abandon their heritage as children of Abraham, those who had been denied their birthright struggled to come to terms with their new situation. Significantly, in John's Gospel the term "the Jews" is used negatively for Jesus' enemies—while there is no corresponding term for Jesus' followers. Johannine believers do not understand themselves to be "Christians," i.e., members of a new religious movement. Those who own the title "Jews" deny them the designation—but the children of light know that they alone are the true children of Abraham.

Matthew may be understood in the same setting, as W. D. Davies and Krister Stendahl have argued.[6] Matthew's Gospel is both Jewish and intensely anti-Jewish. The Pharisees appear as implacable foes throughout the Gospel, mirroring not the situation during Jesus' ministry but when the author composed his Gospel. Matthew's Sermon on the Mount, Davies argues, was intended as a response to the developing interpretation of the Torah in the official rabbinic academy at Jabneh. Jesus, not the Pharisees, is the authorized interpreter of the law. Stendahl demonstrated that behind the Gospel of Matthew is a history of scholarly interpretation of the Scriptures, perhaps even a community of scholars much like a rabbinic school—"scribe[s] who [have] been trained for the kingdom of heaven," as Matthew terms them (Matt. 13:52). Like the author of the fourth Gospel, Matthew wrote in response to upheavals within the larger Jewish community, upheavals occasioned by the disastrous war against Rome and the destruction of the temple.

The war against Rome had an enormous impact on the character of Judaism. Some Jews were unable to survive the loss of the temple. Aristocratic priests who operated the elaborate temple cultus lost their base of power and their livelihood. The conservative element, committed to an understanding of tradition that offered no flexibility in dealing with the changed situation, was simply defined out of the community later. Jews who did survive the war as Jews, on the other hand, began to find plurality an increasing problem as national symbols disappeared. Jews living in the diaspora had long ago recognized that survival depended upon maintaining distinctiveness. The temple's destruction, however, seemed to spawn heightened discomfort about threats to the way of life that set Jews apart from Gentiles. Teachers sought to provide a new ideology that could explain why God's elect had been driven from their land and temple, but they also sought to safeguard the community by providing a more restricted definition of "Jew." Momentum gradually built to exclude from the community elements that threatened to blur the lines of demarcation between Jew and non-Jew. Messianists were apparently among those excluded from the family. Traces of the purge are visible in John and Matthew, accounting for the hostility in both works toward Jews.

It is not difficult to understand the immense literary production generated by the devastating wars against Rome. It is also not difficult to understand why Christian Jews required books of their own. In addition to the general chaos within the community, they had been excluded from the family of faith. They no longer had a place to stand. Questions were inevitable: who are we? where do we come from? do we have any roots? what are our prospects? Teachers obliged to answer such questions could not simply argue that Jesus' people were part of a new religion. The God who raised Jesus from the dead was the God of Abraham, Isaac, and Jacob. Jesus was confessed as Messiah—Israel's Messiah. To make of Christianity a new religion would, as Marcion understood a half-century later, entail belief in a new god, and the consequent rejection of Israel's God and Scriptures. That was a move Christian Jews were unable to make.

When read in the context of this history, Luke-Acts, like Matthew and John, seems to make most sense as a pastoral word addressed to Jewish Christians. For such people, cut adrift from their heritage, the two-volume history would have offered a renewed sense of their identity as God's people. In such a setting, the case Luke set out to argue would not have been the legitimacy of a sense of newness and discontinuity with the past, but rather the appropriateness of the claim of messianists to represent the true Israel. Of course life for Jews who believed in Jesus had changed drastically from the early days by the time Luke wrote. Jerusalem was no longer the center of the earth; Gentiles were flooding into the church; relations with other Jews were troubled. In the face of all contrary evidence, however, Luke-Acts argued that the history of Jesus and his followers belonged within the history of God's people, Israel. From beginning to end, the story is about divine promises fulfilled—about what has been "accomplished among us" (Luke 1:1). Luke's history is about continuity. As he viewed it, human events were the arena not of blind and capricious forces but of God's providence. "Necessity" was a category basic to his view of history.[7] What had occurred, he insisted, had been ordained by a God whose primary attribute was faithfulness to promises.

Some have employed the category "salvation history" to describe Luke's conception. The term is somewhat misleading and probably unnecessary. For Luke, history was saving only in that it was part of the one history of salvation known to the people of God, the history of Israel. Luke wrote about pious Jews confident in a God who keeps his word. Though life brings surprises—like the inclusion of Gentiles, the rejection of Israel's leaders, and the destruction of Jerusalem—it still remains the arena for accomplishing God's purposes and for demonstrating his faithfulness.

There is precedent for Luke's work. Centuries before, Israel's historians had undertaken the task of updating the national story, dealing with changes that called into question the people's self-understanding. Partisans of the monarchy, under the patronage of the court, wrote a new history of God's people to explain how the federation of tribes had given birth to a monarchy, an institutional anathema to the tribes not long before. God's choice of David and the centralization of worship in Jerusalem dominate one version of the national story that found its way into the Scriptures. Again centuries later, when David's kingdom had split and each half had fallen to foreign powers, historians updated the national saga, discerning the movement of God's hand in events that seemed devoid of a divine presence, insisting that God had not finished with the people. Like his contemporary Josephus, Luke wrote for Jews forced to come to terms with a new world in which God's providence was less apparent, a world that witnessed the demise of the temple and the eventual loss of the Jewish homeland.

Luke-Acts fits well into the corpus of crisis literature produced within the Jewish community during the last decades of the first century. In some important respects, however, the dynamics within the community for whom Luke wrote were different from those in the Matthean and Johannine communities. If, as seems likely, Luke wrote for Jewish Christians, the tone of his work is remarkably mild. There is little of the hurt and bitterness reflected in Matthew and John, none of the savagery reserved for the Pharisees or "the Jews."

Two explanations are possible. The first is that Luke wrote before a final schism within the Jewish community, when the prospect of communication between messianists and non-messianists still existed. This case is argued by David Tiede. He locates the complete break between "Christians" and "Jews" later, perhaps not until after the Bar Kochba Revolt in 132 C.E. Though the author does not conceal hostilities within the Jewish community toward Jesus' partisans, the positive view of Pharisees in Acts and the negative portrayal of Sadducees may reflect a desire to play down differences between Jesus' followers and other Pharisaic Jews.

Arguing that faith is still to be found within Israel, Luke may hold out some hope of accommodation—or at least of persuading non-believers.

The second explanation, more likely in my view, is that Luke-Acts was written when the separation between messianists and non-messianists was an accomplished fact. It is difficult to read the ending of Acts without sensing the close of an era and an irreconcilable break. The situation may even account for the point at which Luke chooses to end his story. He ends at the conclusion of the mission to Israel, symbolically completed by Paul at Rome, on the verge of the "time of the Gentiles."

Further, the mode of biblical interpretation in Acts is singular in the New Testament, betraying none of the "sectarian" features characteristic of exegesis in Paul's letters, or the Gospels of Matthew and John.[8] Luke's use of Scriptures is closer to that of the apologists in the second century than to that of other New Testament authors. Much like the rabbis, he displays great confidence in the ability of reasonable people to arrive at a proper understanding of the Bible. Yet the content of such "proper understanding of the Bible" differs little from what we find in John or Paul or Matthew. The results of Luke's exegesis are quite thoroughly partisan and "Christian." His confidence in the clarity of Scripture thus seems to betray a different situation; it seems more fitting for an established institution which, like later rabbinic academies, had a firm hold on its adherents, a persuasive ideology, and a scholarly mechanism sufficient to deal with threats to the faith. The reason there is so little hostility toward unbelieving Jews in Acts may be that they pose no serious threat to Luke's audience. The Jewish Christians for whom he wrote may well have been separated from other Jews for some time.

It is thus conceivable that the primary motivation for the composition of Luke-Acts arose not from the outside but from within the believing community. Conzelmann argued that Luke wrote to offer an interpretation of history for third-generation Christians. He may be correct. The audience was principally Jewish-Christian, however—people who may have come to terms with their separation from the larger Jewish community but who required clarification about their own circumstances within the church. The flood of Gentiles pouring into congregations and the end of large-scale conversions of Jews perhaps raised questions about their heritage. Perhaps Luke's history was an effort to confirm their identity as the people of God, to bolster their flagging confidence that their gospel was secure and well-founded. That is, of course, what Luke claimed he would do in his introduction.

Perceiving Luke as an address to Jewish Christians need not limit its subject matter to "religious" concerns narrowly conceived. Jews had long been members of a hellenized world and, at the time Luke wrote, a world under the sway of Caesars. Fred Danker and David Tiede have both argued that Luke's rhetoric was intended also as a critique of competing claims of so-called saviors within the larger Roman world.[9] David Tiede writes:

> The grand sweep and propositions of Luke's narrative do evoke its larger cultural setting, especially since the courage and confidence with which Luke assured his readers were then in short supply among the victors as well as the vanquished. The glorious promise of the golden age of Augustus, with the savior-benefactors manifesting the generosity of divine providence for all humanity, was now often perceived as empty, if not false, prophecy. Abuses of power, followed by assassinations and coups within the imperial ranks, disruptions of social structures, and ensuing economic chaos threatened to produce a failure of nerve in which many duty-bound Romans would languish. Therefore, Luke's mission theology as a messianist scriptural commentary and critique of such imperial rhetoric and ideology merits considerably more attention. Clearly, Luke does intend to equip the church to come to terms with that vast political, philosophical, and religious discussion by means of an audacious vision of God's providence through the exalted messiah and Lord, Jesus.[10]

Uncertainties remain, and students of the Gospel and Acts will continue to debate the merits of different theories about the author and his audience and the purpose of his books. About some matters we can be confident, however. Luke-Acts was not composed as missionary literature. Its primary function was internal. Through his writings the author sought to provide meaning and security to believers in troubled times. The medium he chose was historical narrative. Though Luke-Acts may not fit neatly the canons of historiography in the hellenistic world, Jewish histories—biblical and non-biblical—provide the most instructive parallels. Perhaps Luke even conceived of himself as a sort of biblical historian, carrying the story of God's people into a new era.[11]

It is significant that Luke chose history as the medium through which to address his generation. Many of the past debates about whether or not Luke was really a "historian" had to do with questions about the accuracy of his narrative. Such questions have their place, but they tend to obscure the real significance of Luke's undertaking. History, after all, is less a matter of data than of patterns and themes. Historiographers are people who seek to make sense of a confusing welter of human experience by arranging experiences into some discernible order, detecting coherences and connections. Like perception, history requires some notion of order and structure. Luke, furthermore, wrote religious history—a history that dared to offer readers a sense of meaning in a universe with ultimate significance. Luke's reason for offering his own version of the story was perhaps less in order to set the record straight than to extend Christian claims into the whole arena of human experience. His boldness and the scope of his undertaking merit our admiration.

Luke sought to help his audience make sense of their lives by telling them a story. He provided a framework in which they could locate themselves and in which they could find meaning. That is precisely the function of religion in human society, as Peter Berger has so clearly argued.[12] Religion, he explains, is a natural response of human beings to a cosmos that is always threatening. In some societies simple religious beliefs suffice in warding off the demons. Elaborate religious systems and religious literature are not required by people whose simple lives involve no serious challenge to traditional ways and common assumptions. Disruption, however, brings the validity of one's way of life into question. When such disruption occurs, a community requires an ordered system of symbols capable of explaining the challenges to traditional ways in terms of the traditional. The alternative would be to abandon any sense of wholeness and consistency and to surrender to relativism and chaos—an intolerable alternative. Human beings cannot survive without a "sacred canopy" over life to ward off the threat of the demons:

> The socially established nomos may thus be understood, perhaps in its most important aspect, as a shield against terror. Put differently, the most important function of society is nomization. The anthropological presupposition for this is a human craving for meaning that appears to have the force of instinct.[13]

Whatever our precise interpretation of Luke's message, we can understand what the author sought to do for his community. We distort the function of his history if we speak only of Luke's soteriology or his Christology. Luke wrote to create a sense of order, to impose on experience a pattern. Bolder than most, he set out to provide meaning by locating himself and his community within the framework of a story that began with the call of Abraham and would end only with the return of Christ to gather his elect from the four winds. In the story of the circumcised believers—and only there—was the guiding hand of Israel's God to be seen.

To some, Luke's whole enterprise might seem scandalously one-sided. Writing for a religious minority, new on the scene, his writings cannot, however, be termed triumphalistic, a charge frequently leveled at Luke-Acts.[14] The narrator's confidence in the ability of people to perceive the truth may be naive; his understanding of suffering may well lack depth. The audacity of his claims, however, and the breadth of his undertaking are breathtaking.

At a time in history when there is little boldness among philosophers and historiographers, when in church and society teachers are content with analysis and critique, Luke-Acts may serve as a reminder of a larger task. Human experience may resist our attempts at systematization and control, but detached cynicism is a luxury we can ill afford. A refusal to look for causes and connections in human affairs may serve to conceal our own complicity in the ills of the world and to offer an escape from active involvement in efforts to create a more just and peaceable society.

Our age, like the age in which Luke wrote, has witnessed sweeping changes and social upheavals. The world has become more complex and confusing. Ordering mechanisms do not seem to work. Societies drift toward totalitarianism or collapse into chaos. Families disintegrate, lives are fragmented, traditions destroyed. We cannot live with chaos. We need a philosophy, a workable social order, and an ability to appreciate God's providential ordering of the creation. We require a sense of the larger history of which we are a part, a history whose beginning and whose end are in the hands of a God who will ultimately triumph over the forces of darkness.

Luke's optimism may be naive. Yet in our time, in a society where Christians have real power or access to power, abandoning creation to the forces of darkness would be a premature surrender. The apocalyptic mentality is more dangerous, perhaps, than naive optimism. It is willing to consider the possibility of nuclear holocaust, and its preoccupation with crises of cosmic proportion can conceal the small wounds we regularly inflict on creation. And even if we possess power, sensing genuine possibilities in our future requires confidence that life makes sense, that the past contains resources for the present, that we can believe in a God who is dependable and can be trusted with our destiny. Like Theophilus, we need to know that what we have been taught is "well-founded."

NOTES

Introduction

1. On the use of titles in Graeco-Roman literature, see M. Dibelius, "The First Christian Historian," *Studies in the Acts of the Apostles*, ed. H. Greeven, trans. M. Ling (New York: Charles Scribner's Sons, 1956), pp. 135-6; Henry J. Cadbury, *The Making of Luke-Acts* (London: S.P.C.K., 1958), pp. 195-6.
2. Ernst Haenchen, *The Acts of the Apostles*, trans. B. Noble and G. Shinn (Philadelphia: Westminster Press, 1971), pp. 50-60.
3. Cadbury's *The Making of Luke-Acts* was first published in 1927.
4. On sources, see Haenchen, *Acts*, pp. 81-90.
5. A persistent critic of Markan priority has been William R. Farmer, *The Synoptic Problem* (New York: Macmillan, 1964).
6. The Greek word for "gospel" means "good message." Paul uses the term to designate the message of salvation in Jesus (see 1 Cor. 15:1–7). The noun does not appear in Luke's "Gospel." The use of the term as a designation for a book is late, perhaps toward the end of the second century. See note 1 above.
7. Haechen, *Acts*, pp. 112-116; Philipp Vielhauer, "On the 'Paulinism' of Acts," *Studies in Luke-Acts*, ed. Leander E. Keck and J. Louis Martyn (Nashville: Abingdon, 1966), pp. 33-50.
8. Henry J. Cadbury, "The Diction of Luke and Acts," *The Style and Literary Method of Acts* (Cambridge, Mass.: Harvard University Press, 1920).
9. On the dating of Mark, see my *An Introduction to New Testament Literature* (Nashville: Abingdon, 1978), pp. 146-150 and 196-98, or Werner Georg Kümmel, *Introduction to the New Testament*, 14th ed., trans. A. J. Mattill, Jr. (Nashville: Abingdon, 1966), pp. 70-71.
10. For a discussion of the various possibilities, see Haenchen, *Acts*, pp. 144-46.

11. For a thorough discussion of the date and place of the composition of Luke-Acts, see Joseph A. Fitzmyer, *The Gospel According to Luke, I-IX,* ANCHOR BIBLE 28 (Garden City: Doubleday, 1981), pp. 53-57.

CHAPTER I

1. The foremost of such commentators is Hans Conzelmann, who stated in his well known study of Luke that since "the authenticity of these first two chapters is questionable, we have not taken into account the statements that are peculiar to them." *The Theology of St. Luke,* trans. G. Buswell (New York: Harper and Row, 1960), p. 117.

2. See the suggestive essay by Paul Minear, "Luke's Use of the Birth Stories," *Studies in Luke-Acts,* pp. 111-130.

3. Flavius Josephus, *The Life Against Apion,* LOEB CLASSICAL LIBRARY, 8 vols., trans. Henry Thackeray (Cambridge, Mass.: Harvard University Press, 1966), 1:163-5, 293-5.

4. Information about the use of speeches in histories is provided by Martin Dibelius, "The Speeches in Acts and Ancient Historiography," *Studies in the Acts of the Apostles,* pp. 138-185, and in Henry J. Cadbury, "The Speeches in Acts," *The Beginnings of Christianity,* ed. F. J. Foakes Jackson and Kirsopp Lake (London: Macmillan, 1920-33), 5:401-427.

5. The case is argued by Cadbury, *The Making of Luke-Acts,* pp. 344-348 and 358-359.

6. For a thorough discussion of the source question, see Fitzmyer, *Luke,* pp. 63-106.

7. The quotations are taken from David R. Cartlidge and David L. Dungan, *Documents for the Study of the Gospels* (Philadelphia: Fortress, 1980), pp. 131-133.

8. For a helpful discussion of Simeon's oracle and its programmatic significance, see David Tiede, *Prophecy and History in Luke-Acts* (Philadelphia: Fortress, 1980), pp. 24-31.

CHAPTER II

1. For a detailed analysis of the scene, see Tiede, *Prophecy and History,* chapter 2.

2. For an introduction to form-criticism, see Martin Dibelius, *From Tradition to Gospel,* trans. B. L. Woolf (New York: Scribner's, 1935), and Rudolf Bultmann, *The History of the Synoptic Tradition,* trans. J. Marsh (New York: Harper and Row, 1963). Also helpful is Edgar V.

McKnight, *What Is Form Criticism?* (Philadelphia: Fortress Press, 1969). For a recent work, Arland J. Hultgren, *Jesus and His Adversaries* (Minneapolis: Augsburg, 1979).

3. Dibelius, *From Tradition to Gospel*, commented that the evangelists should be viewed as "collectors, vehicles of tradition, editors" (p. 3).

4. See Norman Perrin, *What Is Redaction Criticism?* (Philadelphia: Fortress, 1969). For a brief analysis of the shift in biblical scholarship to a more literary approach to Gospel studies, see my *An Introduction to New Testament Literature*, chapter 2.

5. A. Jülicher, *Die Gleichnisreden Jesu* (Tübingen: J. C. B. Mohr, 1899).

6. C. H. Dodd, *The Parables of the Kingdom* (London: Nisbet, 1935).

7. Joachim Jeremias, *The Parables of Jesus,* trans. S. H. Hooke (New York: Scribner's, 1963).

8. Robert W. Funk, *Language, Hermeneutic, and Word of God* (New York: Harper and Row, 1966).

9. Apollonius lived during the second half of the first century. His biographer, Flavius Philostratus, wrote around 218 C.E., using in his work traditions preserved by Apollonius' disciples.

10. The translation is from Cartlidge and Dungan, *Documents for the Study of the Gospels,* p. 231.

11. Howard M. Teeple, *The Mosaic Eschatological Prophet* (Philadelphia: Society of Biblical Literature, 1957).

12. The source of such traditions about persecuted and martyred prophets is unclear, but traditions were current in pre-Christian times. Josephus, the Jewish historian, reports such stories about Manasseh (*Antiquities* 10.3.1; see also 9.13.2). The material is collected in a German work by H. J. Schoeps, *Die Jüdischen Prophetenmorde* (Uppsala: Max Niehans, 1943). See also the introduction to "The Martyrdom of Isaiah," in R. H. Charles, *Apocrypha and Pseudepigrapha of the Old Testament* (Oxford: Clarendon Press, 1913) pp. 2, 155-8.

13. In light of reliable manuscript evidence, the traditional word of Jesus from the cross, "Father, forgive them. . . ." must be judged a later addition to Luke's Gospel.

14. Josephus offers two unflattering portraits of Pilate in *Antiquities* 18:55-58, and in *Jewish Wars* 2:169-177.

15. See the work by Charles H. Talbert, *Luke and the Gnostics,* (Nashville: Abingdon, 1966).

16. See especially Paul Schubert, "The Structure and Significance of Luke 24," *Neutestamentliche Studien für Rudolf Bultmann* (Berlin: Töpelmann, 1954), pp. 165-186.

Chapter III

1. See Haenchen, *Acts*, pp. 144-46.
2. For information about the Jewish festival (The Feast of Booths), see Theodore H. Gaster, *Festivals of the Jewish Year* (New York: Morrow, 1952-3). For a discussion of the passage and an extensive bibliography, Haenchen, *Acts*, pp. 172-75.
3. The evidence from Philo and from rabbinic sources is conveniently summarized in Kirsopp Lake, "The Gift of the Spirit on the Day of Pentecost," *Beginnings of Christianity* 5: 114-16.
4. Ibid.
5. See chapter 1, note 1, above.
6. For a review of current scholarship, Joseph A. Fitzmyer, "Der semitische Hintergrund des neutestmentlichen Kyriostitels," *Jesus Christus in Historie und Theologie*, ed. G. Strecker (Tübingen: J. C. B. Mohr, 1975), pp. 267-298. The essay is now in English in his *A Wandering Aramean: Collected Aramaic Essays* (Missoula: Scholars Press, 1979), pp. 115-42.
7. For a discussion of the interpretive moves made in the speech, see my "The Use of Psalm 16 in Acts 2," *Catholic Biblical Quarterly* 43 (1981):543-556.
8. Jacob Jervell, "James: The Defender of Paul," *Luke and the People of God* (Minneapolis: Augsburg, 1972), pp. 185-199.
9. My interpretation of Stephen's speech is heavily indebted to an essay by Nils Alstrup Dahl, "The Story of Abraham in Luke-Acts," *Jesus in the Memory of the Early Church* (Minneapolis: Augsburg, 1976), pp. 66-86.
10. The case is argued vigorously by J. Knox in his *Chapters in a Life of Paul* (Nashville: Abingdon, 1950).
11. This detail is all the more striking in that Paul discusses eating meat offered to idols in 1 Cor. 8—10. The Jewish law is not even a consideration in the rather lengthy discussion. It is possible that such a decree was issued, but that it derives from some time after the Jerusalem conference. Perhaps the decree was in some measure motivated by the conference. Luke's information may be somewhat confused. See Dibelius, "The Apostolic Council," *Studies in the Acts of the Apostles*, pp. 93-101. For more of the background of Luke's views, see chapter 5, note 9 below.
12. See the discussion in Dibelius, "The Acts of the Apostles in the Setting of the History of Early Christian Literature," *Studies in the Acts of the Apostles*, pp. 196-206.

13. The thematic importance of Paul's suffering in Acts is the subject of a book by David Adams soon to appear from Fortress Press.

14. See the commentary on Habakkuk (IQpHab) in G. Vermes, *The Dead Sea Scrolls in English* (Baltimore: Penguin Books, 1962), pp. 232-240.

15. The primary motivation for Paul's trip to Jerusalem was to deliver the collection he had gathered from his churches, a matter of considerable political significance. Paul viewed the acceptance of the collection by the Jerusalem church as an affirmation of his ministry and an acknowledgment of the unity of Jewish and Gentile Christian congregations. Paul knew he was likely to encounter resistance (see Rom. 15:30–33). Luke seems to have known little about the collection or its importance.

16. Jacob Jervell, "Paul: The Teacher of Israel," *Luke and the People of God,* pp. 153-184.

CHAPTER IV

1. See L. Johnson, *The Literary Function of Possessions in Luke-Acts,* SBL DISSERTATION SERIES 39 (Missoula: Scholars Press, 1977).

2. Ibid, pp. 2-3.

3. The translation is from Herbert Danby, *The Mishnah* (Oxford: Oxford University Press, 1933), p. 446.

4. From John G. Gager, *Kingdom and Community* (Englewood Cliffs, N.J.: Prentice-Hall, 1975), p. 131.

5. On Montanus and his followers, see the discussion in Hans von Campenhausen, *Ecclesiastical Authority and Spiritual Power in the Church of the First Three Centuries,* trans. J. A. Baker (Stanford: Stanford University Press, 1969).

6. There is a fine collection of material on Simon Magus, the arch-heretic, in Robert P. Casey, "Simon Magus," *The Beginnings of Christianity* 5:151-163.

7. See my "The Use of Psalm 16 in Acts 2," and William Stephen Kurz, "The Function of Christological Proof from Prophecy for Luke and Justin" (Ph.D. Dissertation, Yale University, 1976).

8. It is interesting that scholars like Conzelmann and Haenchen, who have devoted much of their professional lives to the study of Lukan writings, regard Luke's theological perspective as inadequate.

9. Tiede, *Prophecy and History in Luke-Acts.*

CHAPTER V

1. Kümmel, *Introduction,* p. 115.

2. Howard Clark Kee, Franklin W. Young, and Karlfried Froehlich,

Understanding the New Testament, 2nd ed. (Englewood Cliffs, N.J.: Prentice-Hall, 1965), p. 322.

3. Conzelmann, *The Theology of St. Luke,* p. 165.

4. The two essays by Dahl in *Jesus and the Memory of the Early Church* ("The Story of Abraham in Luke-Acts" and "The Purpose of Luke-Acts") and Jervell's collection of essays in *Luke and the People of God* have been among the most influential publications. Tiede's *Prophecy and History in Luke-Acts* and Johnson's *The Literary Function of Possessions in Luke-Acts* carry the arguments further.

5. For Conzelmann's views, see note 1, chapter 1, above.

6. The so-called "Great Omission," Luke's failure to include material from Mark 6:45—8:27 in his Gospel, has been the subject of considerable speculation. We may at least note that because he omits such material from his Gospel, Luke gives no impression that Jesus left the region of Galilee. See Conzelmann, *The Theology of St. Luke,* pp. 52-55.

7. The contrast with Galatians 2 is particularly striking. There, Paul states that he "had been entrusted with the gospel to the uncircumcised, just as Peter had been entrusted with the gospel to the circumcised" (2:7). There is no indication that Peter had anything to do with the Gentile mission.

8. James is known in Christian tradition as a Jewish Christian who had the respect of the Jewish community. See Jervell, "James: Defender of Paul," *Luke and the People of God,* pp. 185-199.

9. There is a reflection here of discussions in Jewish circles about relations with non-Jews and what could be expected of them. There may be some connection with traditions about "Noachian" commandments (the laws given to Noah in Gen. 9 that apply to all peoples). See the comments in the Babylonian Talmud, *Sanhedrin* 56 a-b.

10. G. F. Moore, *Judaism in the First Centuries of the Christian Era: The Age of the Tannaim,* 3 vols. (Cambridge, Mass.: Harvard University Press, 1927-30); H. J. Schoeps, *Paul: The Theology of the Apostle in the Light of Jewish Religious History,* trans. H. Knight (Philadelphia: Westminster, 1961); E. P. Sanders, *Paul and Palestinian Judaism* (Philadelphia: Fortress, 1977).

11. On Luke's view of the law, see Jervell, "The Law in Luke-Acts," *Luke and the People of God,* pp. 133-152; on Paul's view, see W. Gutbrod's essay in *Theological Dictionary of the New Testament,* ed. and trans. Geoffrey W. Bromiley (Grand Rapids, Mich.: Eerdmans, 1967),

4:1065-1078, as well as standard works on Paul by Rudolf Bultmann,
Günther Bornkam, and Ernst Käsemann.

CHAPTER VI

1. For some sense of the new directions in the study of Jewish
   backgrounds, see the numerous volumes by Jacob Neusner devoted to
   a form-critical assessment of rabbinic traditions, the two volumes of
   essays edited by E. P. Sanders, *Jewish and Christian Self-Definition*
   (Philadelphia: Fortress, 1980-81) and Nils Alstrup Dahl, "Eschatology
   and History in Light of the Qumran Texts," *The Crucified Messiah*
   (Minneapolis: Augsburg, 1974), pp. 129-145.
2. Günter Klein, *Die Zwölf Apostel* (Göttingen: Vandenhoeck und
   Ruprecht, 1961).
3. Haenchen, *Acts*, pp. 106, 622, 693-4.
4. Hans Conzelmann, *The Theology of St. Luke*, and "Luke's Place in the
   Development of Early Christianity," *Studies in Luke-Acts*, pp.
   298-316.
5. J. Louis Martyn, *History and Theology in the Fourth Gospel* (New
   York: Harper, 1968); Raymond Brown, *The Gospel According to
   John*, ANCHOR BIBLE 29 and 29a (Garden City, N.Y.: Doubleday, 1970),
   and *The Community of the Beloved Disciple* (Ramsey, N.J.: Paulist
   Press, 1979).
6. William David Davies, *The Setting of the Sermon on the Mount*
   (Cambridge: Cambridge University Press, 1964). K. Stendahl, *The
   School of St. Matthew* (Philadelphia: Fortress Press, 1968).
7. Tiede locates the discussion of "necessity" within a Jewish prophetic
   framework and within larger discussions of fate and providence in the
   Graeco-Roman world. See *Prophecy and History*, pp. 27-33.
8. See my "Use of Psalm 16 in Acts 2," and Kurz, "The Function of
   Christological Proof from Prophecy."
9. Frederick W. Danker, *Jesus and the New Age* (St. Louis: Clayton
   Publishing House, 1972) and *Luke* (Philadelphia: Fortress Press,
   1976).
10. Tiede, *Prophecy and History*, p. 132.
11. Dahl, "The Purpose of Luke-Acts," p. 88.
12. Peter L. Berger and Thomas Luckmann, *The Social Construction of
    Reality* (Garden City, N.Y.: Doubleday, 1966) and Peter L. Berger,
    The Sacred Canopy (Garden City, N.Y.: Doubleday, 1967).
13. Berger, *The Sacred Canopy*, p. 22.
14. Tiede, *Prophecy and History*, pp. 129-30. The charge may be
    appropriate to later use of Lukan writings in Christian tradition.

SELECTED BIBLIOGRAPHY

Barrett, C. K. *Luke the Historian in Recent Study.* London: The Epworth Press, 1961, 76 pp.
Barrett deals with some of the questions of text, historiography, Semitisms, sources and ecclesiology involved in Luke-Acts. He provides a helpful overview of the arguments of Dibelius, Morgenthaler, Conzelmann, Haenchen, *et al,* and gives his own assessment of Luke-Acts in the context of early Christianity.

Cadbury, Henry J. *The Making of Luke-Acts.* London: S.P.C.K., 1927, reprinted 1958, 385 pp.
As the title indicates, Cadbury attempts to recover the factors involved in the literary process that produced Luke and Acts. He does so by considering: 1) materials—forms and sources; 2) common methods—contemporary literary types and conventions, especially with reference to Greek and Hellenistic literature; 3) personality of the author; and 4) purpose of the author—the legitimacy of Christianity to both Jews and Gentiles and a defense of Christianity in light of Roman law. The book is a classic.

Conzelmann, Hans. *The Theology of St. Luke,* trans. G. Buswell. New York: Harper and Row, 1960, 255 pp.
The German title of this work, *Die Mitte der Zeit,* indicates more clearly Conzelmann's main point. Writing in response to the delay of the parousia, Luke identified the period of Jesus' ministry as the center of history, preceded by the period of Israel and followed by the period of the church. Conzelmann's study was a pioneering venture in redaction criticism.

Danker, Frederick, W. *Luke.* Philadelphia: Fortress, 1976, 120 pp.
Danker is conscious of Luke's problem of communicating God's merciful benefactions, rooted in Jewish tradition, to a contemporary Roman-Hellenistic civilization. Luke's solution, according to Danker, is to present Jesus as a Hellenistic benefactor. Danker draws out the

implications of such a portrayal, discussing features of Lukan ethics, the use of prophetic motifs, and the aim of the structured form of Luke's Gospel.

Dibelius, Martin. *Studies in the Acts of the Apostles.* London: SCM Press Ltd, 1956, 228 pp.
This book is a collection of eleven essays by Dibelius. In these essays, Dibelius deals with history and historiography in Acts, form critical concerns, and the figure of Paul in Acts among other topics. He is also concerned with setting Acts not only in the context of the early church but also in relation to other Greek and Latin authors.

Ellis, E. Earle, *The Gospel of Luke.* The Century Bible. London: Nelson, 1966, 300 pp.
In this commentary, Ellis emphasizes the accuracy and historicity of Luke and is concerned with his theology. Luke, he argues, writes to refute de-historicizing Gnostics, to provide a correct eschatology, and to deal with the relationship of Judaism and Christianity. Ellis gives attention to structure and theme, the Jewish background, and the use of Scripture. The volume provides helpful special notes and a good bibliography.

Fitzmyer, Joseph. *The Gospel According to Luke, I-IX.* ANCHOR BIBLE 28. Garden City, N.Y.: Doubleday, 1981, 837 pp.
The first volume of Prof. Fitzmyer's commentary on the first nine chapters of Luke's Gospel offers massive testimony to the erudition of its author. The 258-page introduction offers a survey of Lukan scholarship, and as expected, the bibliography is thorough.

Foakes, Jackson, F. J. and Kirsopp Lake. *The Beginnings of Christianity.* 5 vols. London: Macmillan, 1920-1933.
This five volume work is a treasury of information about the Acts of the Apostles. Volume 1 investigates the Jewish, Gentile, and Christian backgrounds. Volume 2 deals with the questions of the composition and authorship of Acts and the history of their treatment by other critics. Volume 3 is a critical study of the text. Volume 4 is a translation and commentary (Lake and Cadbury, eds.) with additional notes in Volume 5.

Haenchen, Ernst. *The Acts of the Apostles,* trans. H. Anderson. Philadelphia: Westminster Press, 1971, 737 pp.
Haenchen introduces this commentary with an extensive background of the history of use and study of Acts. He sees the purpose of Acts to be a

political apology to Rome and a mission effort to the Gentiles who no longer live under the law. The commentary is divided into sixty-eight pericopes with a large bibliography for each pericope.

Interpretation 27 (April, 1973)
This volume of *Interpretation* deals exclusively with Acts. There are articles by Paul Minear on kerygmatic intention and claim, by George W. MacRae on Christology, by F. F. Bruce on the Holy Spirit, and by Leander E. Keck on Acts 1:8.

Interpretation 30 (October, 1976)
This volume of *Interpretation* deals exclusively with Luke. There are articles by Frederick W. Danker on the use of Luke in the lectionaries, by Arland J. Hultgren on interpreting Luke, by Ralph P. Martin on salvation and discipleship, and by Charles H. Talbert on Luke in recent study.

Jervell, Jacob. *Luke and the People of God.* Minneapolis: Augsburg Publishing House, 1972, 207 pp.
This book consists of seven essays which deal with Lukan ecclesiology: the relation of the church to Israel and the Gentiles and the problem of the Jewish rejection of the church. In contrast to widely held opinions, Jervell does not see Luke-Acts to be an apology for an institutional church nor an address to a Gentile community.

Marshall, I. Howard. *Commentary on Luke.* Grand Rapids: Eerdmans, 1978, 928 pp.
This book is a commentary on the Greek text of Luke, yet is not too technical. There is a large general bibliography as well as bibliographies for each pericope. This volume thus provides access to much of the recent study on Luke. Marshall employs historical-critical methods and also attempts to understand Luke theologically.

Perspectives on Luke-Acts, ed. Charles H. Talbert. Danville, Va.: Association of Baptist Professors of Religion, 1978.
This book is a product of a five-year study group on Luke and Acts. There are fifteen essays by many noted scholars. The book is divided into two parts: "Introductory Issues," and "Studies of Forms, Sections, and Themes."

Studies in Luke-Acts, eds. Leander E. Keck and J. Louis Martyn. Philadelphia: Fortress Press, 1980, 316 pp.
This book consists of nineteen essays which reflect a broad spectrum of

perspectives and the history of study of Luke-Acts in the recent past. Topics include the place of Luke-Acts in the early church, the portrait of Paul in Acts, Lukan theology, and the relationship of Luke to Acts.

Talbert, Charles H. *Literary Patterns, Theological Themes and the Genre of Luke-Acts.* SBLMS, 20. Missoula, Mont.: Scholars Press, 1974, 159 pp. Talbert insists that an understanding of Luke-Acts must take into account formal patterns. By use of "architecture analysis," he identifies certain key formal patterns in Luke-Acts, shows their relationship to the larger cultural context, and explores their function and relation to theological perspectives.

Tiede, David L. *Prophecy and History in Luke-Acts.* Philadelphia: Fortress Press, 1980, 166 pp. Tiede believes that Luke-Acts reflects the Jewish-Christian community's struggle for identity in light of the destruction of Jerusalem and criticisms from fellow Jews. What Luke wrote was a "gospel for the duration" testifying to God's faithfulness through the Scriptures' fulfillment in the story of Jesus and his followers.

INDEX OF BIBLE PASSAGES